Analytics Interpreted:

A compilation of perspectives

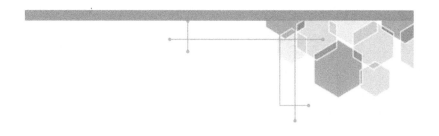

Analytics Interpreted

A compilation of perspectives.

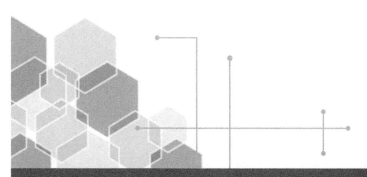

Curated by
REHGAN AVON & DAVE CHERRY

Women in Analytics

Analytics. Featuring Women. For Everyone.

The mission of Women in Analytics is to provide visibility to the women making an impact in the analytics space and a platform for them to lead the conversations around the advancements of analytical research, development, and application.

"I love the mission of the Women in Analytics organization and was honored to be asked to contribute to the WIA book. Collaboration has been a key ingredient to my data and analytics strategies, and I'm hopeful that others will find my point of view helpful in their journey to increase the visibility and influence of data and analytics in their organizations."

Ursula Cottone
Chief Data & Architecture Officer, Huntington Bank

"I have seen firsthand on projects, in the classroom, and in research how women make a positive difference by engaging in data analytics. They offer unique perspectives, thoughtful ideas, and positive attitudes that accelerate progress and generate better results time and again. I am thrilled to participate in efforts like this book that include, inform, and inspire women!"

Barb Wixom
Principal Research Scientist, MIT Sloan Center
for Information Systems Research

"We need more women in data and analytics to foster a more equitable world and to mitigate the risk of bias at scale with AI. It's an honor to support WIA's mission and book in bringing more diversity of thought, inspiration, and best practices to this critical field. As a woman raised primarily by my father, I lacked successful female role models, particularly in tech, and am excited to learn from some of the best voices in the analytics industry."

Cindi Howson
Chief Data Strategy Officer, Thoughtspot

ISBN eBook: 978-1-7365953-1-2
ISBN Paperback: 978-1-7365953-0-5

Edited by Karen Pasley
Layout by Kelley Engelbrecht
Cover design by Sarah Duff

Curator and author photographs courtesy of the individuals.

This book is dedicated to the many amazing, successful women in analytics who are charting the course and inspiring the next generation of leaders; to those up-and-coming women who are currently building momentum in their careers; and to the youngest generation of curious, inquisitive, and bright minds who aspire to be the future leaders in the field of analytics

Table of Contents

Inspiration

Strategy

Ethics

Data Availability

Model Preparation

Data Visualization and Business Intelligence

Case Studies

Rehgan Avon
Founder
Women in Analytics

Preface

The mission of Women in Analytics is to create platforms for more diverse voices to be heard in the analytics space. Diversity of thought is critical in general, but especially in analytics. Our job in analytics is to take information and make sense of it in order to make better-informed decisions. We are trying to simplify the complexity of the world around us to help us explain it for some specific purpose.

A predictive model is a drastically oversimplified representation of past events that we can use to understand the likelihood of different outcomes given specific scenarios. If data, and the way we make sense of it, is meant to get as close to reality as possible, and if reality is viewed through perception, shouldn't we include every angle to ensure we are accurately interpreting it?

The biggest contributor to the failure of analytics is a lack of context. We often don't understand what the data is supposed to mean, what it might be telling us, what relationships exist, or what we should do with it. Analytics is an art just as much as it is a science. It must be challenged, questioned, and tested. Even if an algorithm is extremely accurate, we must understand the implications of how it might be used. All of this to say, diversity of thought is arguably the most important thing we can foster to ensure we use this complex tool properly.

Accomplishing WIA's mission of amplifying diverse voices has not been easy. Let me start by saying, it is not for a lack of finding incredibly impressive and influential diverse individuals. The hard part is getting their voices out.

One challenge is the reluctance to share and be vulnerable. The most frequent response I hear is, "I am not sure I can speak (or write); I am not an expert." Good news: you don't have to be! There is inherent value in sharing your ideas, thoughts, and techniques to solve problems. Others build off of shared experiences and knowledge to make improvements. Without this, we create echo chambers in which the same people say the same thing in the same way. We need to start being OK with being wrong and learning. We need to realize that vulnerability provides growth opportunities for others as well as ourselves.

Delivery matters just as much as the message. We see people sharing ideas through posting on websites, speaking at conferences, or writing articles or papers (or books). All of these are excellent means of communicating your ideas, thoughts, and techniques. Who is listening and how many are listening in part dictates the thought leaders and the experts. This is why WIA spends so much time creating and providing opportunities for talented diverse voices to reach an audience.

This book is another one of those opportunities. Dave and I have had the great privilege of reading the submissions and curating an amazing list of thought leaders discussing the topic we love most: analytics. We hope you enjoy it as much as we did.

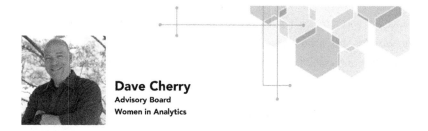

Dave Cherry
Advisory Board
Women in Analytics

Preface

When I first approached Rehgan about this book project, I told her that I had an idea that she was either going to love or hate. I wasn't sure whether she'd like the idea, primarily because of the effort that I knew we'd need to put into it relative to her busy schedule. Given that you are reading this, you know her response. She loved it. I should have known better.

Ever since Rehgan asked me to join the Women in Analytics Advisory Board, I've seen her dedication, leadership, and drive to fulfill the mission of promoting women's voices in analytics. WIA has grown well beyond a simple conference to a thriving and growing community. We've featured amazing speakers whose eager support is so often clearly on display with their enthusiasm. We've educated and upskilled many women through workshops, speaker coaching, and mentoring. And we've continued to create new channels to communicate and connect with the community through social media, webinars, and — now — this book.

Through it all, I've been privileged to meet so many amazing women. In fact, I often feel that my perspective on the gender disparity in the analytics workforce is skewed since I know so many great women leaders. Perhaps the best part of these connections is the authenticity and depth that underlie relationships within the WIA community. Whether data scientists or strategists, individuals bring their expertise and find like-minded colleagues but also appreciate and understand the value of others. Everyone is involved with a growth mindset — seeking growth for themselves and looking for ways to support and enable others.

Just as I wasn't certain of Rehgan's response to this project, I likewise had to wonder about the response we'd get when we put out our call for essay submissions. Again, I should have known better.

There were three things that got me so excited as we started receiving submissions. First, the response of friends was outstanding. Many of the women that I've known professionally and through WIA decided to submit essays. In reading their contributions, I got to know them at another level. Some shared their expertise, while others offered advice and inspiration. But all took the time to support WIA and share their expertise with the goal of helping others succeed. Second, the response from those I didn't know was even more amazing. Many of these women didn't know me, didn't know Rehgan, and likely had just heard of WIA. Yet the response was global: we received submissions from France, Poland, Sweden, the United Kingdom, and the United Arab Emirates. These women identified with our mission and will now be forever included in our community. Finally, the creativity, commitment, resilience, and expertise from this group of authors was so inspiring. There were many times that Rehgan and I would text each other after reading a submission and say, "You've got to read this one — it was awesome."

So now our first book is complete. I'm excited for you to read it and find the authors and essays that resonate most with you — the ones that make you want to text your boss, your team, or your colleagues and say, "You've got to read this."

Thank you, Rehgan, for bringing me into the WIA community and partnering with me on this book. Thank you to all of our authors for sharing your words and wisdom. And thank you to the WIA community: this is for you.

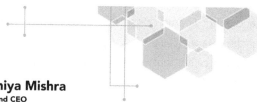

Dr. Taniya Mishra
Founder and CEO
SureStart

Foreward

I am deeply honored to write a foreword for the first data analytics book authored by 45 powerhouse leaders from the Women in Analytics (WIA) community, whose experience, expertise, and empathy (yep, empathy — you need it to do good data analytics for your end users, your customers, and the current and emergent data community) is evident in every page of this book.

I was introduced to Women in Analytics and Rehgan Avon, WIA's awesome founder, in spring 2020, when she kindly invited me as a guest to the virtual speaker series hosted by WIA. From the first email exchange, I knew I was speaking to a kindred spirit. Like me, Rehgan was not only passionate about the various aspects of data analytics, but also wanted to share that passion with a broad community of data enthusiasts — the experts, the newbies, and the curious alike.

The event she invited me to focused on discussing data analytics, careers, and emerging opportunities in the field of voice technology, which has been my sandbox for over a decade. But in prep for the talk, we spent almost as much time talking about community and collaboration. At that time, I had no idea how powerfully — and delightfully — I would see these twin themes of community and collaboration demonstrated in a few months' time in the form of this excellent book on data analytics developed through the collaborative efforts of the WIA community.

This book pulls readers in immediately. Section 1 begins by inspiring us. We right away jump into examples that clearly illustrate how data, harnessed effectively, can lead to data-driven decision-making that impacts both companies and their customers positively. We learn what it takes to embark on a career in the data analytics industry, how to overcome the expected and unexpected challenges life throws our way (very apt at a time when many are going through pandemic-related employment transitions), and how to thrive in our data careers through transparency, a bit of boldness, a listening ear, and continuous learning.

The bright promise of data analytics is complemented in section 2 by an unambiguous acknowledgment of the current state of the industry, in which there continues to be a substantial gap between data analytics and business decision-making. We learn the reasons for this gap and clear strategic steps that can be taken to bridge it. Among the reasons outlined, the one that I personally found the most intriguing had to do with communication — more specifically, storytelling. Storytelling in this context is sharing the most mean-ingful insights derived through the data analytics process to the end users of that analysis in a way that they can easily understand. It requires use of emotional and sensory language that people can relate to, remember, and feel compelled to act upon. But storytelling is not something that computer science or data science curricula, either at the undergraduate or graduate level, often contain. Thus many analysts — though brilliant at technically ana-lyzing the data — are unable to share their insights with decision makers in a way that answers the questions that are of greatest import to the business. The good news is that all analytics teams can develop a culture of storytelling through the adoption, practice, and sharing of the structured thinking and storytelling strategies outlined in this volume.

The second half of the book (sections 4-6) focuses on specifics related to different stages of the data pipeline, including data availability and curation, model preparation, and data visualization. The "what," "why," and "how" related to each of these stages is presented through an easily readable interweaving of stories, advice, and clearly outlined pointers.

Before the book embarks on the proverbial nuts and bolts of data analytics, though, a thoughtful treatment of the ethics surrounding AI development and the data analytics process is presented in section 3. Through examples of recent unfortunate ethical failures in data-based decision-making, the authors discuss the data-related technical reasons for such failures, as well as the frankly more concerning human reasons for them. These include the lack of inclusive teams that represent the community or market the data product or service is built to work in, the failure to proactively consider the human impact of a product/service prior to its development, and the absence of clearly delineated contextual safeguards when estimation- or prediction-based products are deployed. The authors clearly outline the potential mitigations — which do not consist of simply removing obviously bias-related factors like gender. Instead, such mitigations demand both technical safeguards in the form of adoption of new fairness constraints and objective functions, but also ethical considerations that require soul-searching and asking ourselves difficult questions, perhaps including "Should we be building this?"

Through several powerful case studies, the final chapter of the book drives home the message with which section 1 began: data analytics has the potential to bring immense value to companies, to their customers, and even to the broader society. Done right, data analytics can lead to data-informed decision-making that can be transformational for an organization. But to do it "right," the data analytics process must be collaborative, involving all stakeholders from the start; transparent, with open channels for feedback; and innovative, with analysts open to trying new approaches and learning new skills to drive business results.

Overall, I found this book to be deeply insightful, wonderfully readable, and immensely actionable. I expect that the data analytics information, advice, and strategies shared in this volume will be useful to everyone in this field, from novice to expert.

Dr. Taniya Mishra is the founder and CEO of SureStart. She has been an AI scientist for over 10 years, with many peer-reviewed articles, 48 awarded patents, and featured press articles in MIT Technology Review, NBC Learn, and The Atlantic. Taniya was recently recognized for her dedication to mentoring by the WomenTech Network with their prestigious "Mentor of the Year" award for 2020.

Taniya is deeply passionate about increasing AI workforce diversity through opportunity equity. This passion led her to create Affectiva's very popular EMPath AI training program while serving as Affectiva's director of AI Research. Now through SureStart, Taniya's goal is to make this same type of program available to other innovative AI companies that prioritize DEI, so that together they can raise up a new generation of diverse young tech talent.

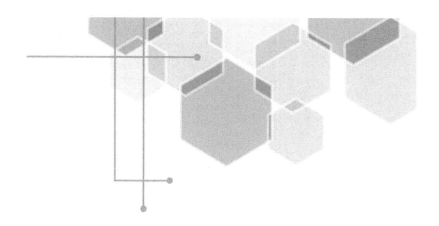

INSPIRATION

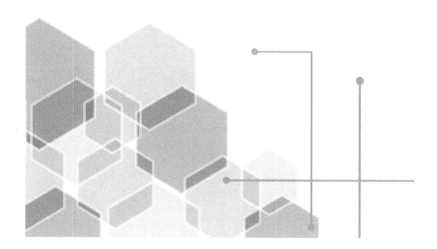

Barb Wixom

Principal Research Scientist at MIT Sloan
Center for Information Systems Research

Creating Value From Data Is Exciting ... When Done Acceptably

2020 marks the 26th year of my academic teaching career. I began at the University of Georgia, teaching databases as a graduate student. Next, I moved to the University of Virginia, where I taught data management, data warehousing, and data strategy as a tenure-track professor. Today, I teach data monetization at the Massachusetts Institute of Technology while serving in the role of principal research scientist. For 26 years, I have taught one consistent message: you need to be creating value from your data!

Initially, this message was a hard sell. At the University of Virginia, I jumped up and down, told dramatic stories, and even rapped to get students excited. The latter manifested as a poorly sung, off-beat rendition of the Sugarhill Gang's "Rapper's Delight" ("Now what you hear is not a test, I'm rapping to the beat…") that could sometimes shock students into excitement. I begged executives to view data as strategic. I tried to convince my dean that data was a skill that all business students needed to learn. He didn't buy it.

In the 1990s, data was a back-office phenomenon that only a handful of companies appreciated. But when companies "got it," they soared. Through research, I studied how First American Corporation used data to transition from "balloons-and-suckers" product marketing to needs-based solutions — and save itself from bankruptcy. I explored how Continental Airlines used data to optimize operations, identify high-value customers, and make pleasing real-time adjustments for those customers — and move from worst to first in the airline industry. I watched Harrah's Casinos use data to deeply understand customer habits and then create tailored coupons, offers, and experiences — and reshape the gaming industry. These inspiring journeys taught me that data mattered, that companies could get data right, and that the rewards for getting data right were huge.

The Data Value Formula

Mistakenly, many companies in the 1990s believed that data value creation was rooted in technology. This belief did not hold up in my research. Regardless of the flavor of the database (a mart, a warehouse, a lake, a lake house), regardless of the flavor of the tech (desktop reporting, Internet of Things, machine learning algorithms, mobile dashboards), regardless of the data at play (images, transactions, social network feeds, sound files, documents, web clickstreams), data value emerged from a consistent formula: compelling need + leadership commitment + behavioral change. If you also added a heavy dash of credible measurement to confirm value realization over time, then you had yourself an exciting success story.

Ultimately, I realized that the heavy dash of measurement is the secret ingredient of data value creation. Essentially what matters to most companies is making money from data. (For nonprofit and government contexts, use the words "mission realization.") If some data project is not clearly making money for the company — or a data investment is not obviously generating returns — the effort will die. And the death is often long, costly, and painful to watch.

Armed with these beliefs, I encouraged people to generate value from data, inside and outside of class. These cheers increasingly resonated, with the renaming of the field from "data warehousing" to "business intelligence," with the promise that companies could "compete on analytics," and with the popularization of the term "data monetization," which directly ties data to money making.

A New Kind of Classroom

By 2012, when the data monetization term was growing hot, I was invited to spend a year conducting research at a nonprofit MIT research center

(MIT CISR) whose mission is to help companies succeed with technology phenomena. I became enthralled with the idea that, through this center, I could expand my reach and help greater numbers of companies generate value from data. After my visiting year ended, I joined MIT CISR as a full-time research scientist.

At MIT CISR, I was blessed with a new kind of classroom, one filled with executives who were highly invested in data value creation. The form of the "classroom" varied from executive education sessions to custom company workshops, to practitioner webinars, to research-based discussions and debates. Regardless of form, this classroom placed me directly in front of business leaders who own and control the "need + commitment + change + measurement" data value formula. It was mind-blowing sometimes to hear about the extraordinary opportunities, hurdles, and pressures these individuals manage every day. These leaders are incredibly smart people with mission-critical jobs. I learned that even they needed cheerleading, if for no other reason than to encourage them to persist with extraordinary efforts.

At MIT CISR, I explore the data value formula within the most complex data contexts that business leaders help me find. My current research includes cross-company data-sharing arrangements, large-scale black-box artificial intelligence (AI) deployments, pervasive data-driven transformation, and selling hard-to-replicate information solutions. I love identifying emergent managerial nuances, such as new collaborative relationships required for data sharing, trust-building activities required for black-box AI, tacit knowledge integration required for data-driven transformation, and value-capture strategies required for selling information. Not only are these nuances interesting to think about, but the better I can help leaders understand and address them, the more time the leaders can devote to the constant care and feeding of essential data value activities.

The Next Frontier: Acceptable Data Value Creation

In 2020, you need to be creating value from your data! It is no longer a hard sell. I don't have to rap; executives naturally interweave data into their strategic plans, and analytics is core to business school curricula. Here's the bad news: through research, I find that as companies use data in more and different ways, they at times can be creepy, hurtful, discriminatory, or damaging. My research suggests that companies can no longer use data with unbridled action — else they offend, let down, ignore, or harm those they need to delight and serve. Companies have transitioned from needing encouragement to create data value to needing encouragement to create data value in acceptable ways.

For now, we don't know how to answer many questions about acceptable data use. We are beginning to understand the importance of involving customers in development processes, running ideas by an array of stakeholder perspectives to spot unintended consequences before they happen, using a devil's advocate to challenge current beliefs, and staffing analytics teams with men and women from diverse races, socioeconomic backgrounds, and geographies. However, it will take years of research to poke and probe and figure out acceptable data use management. My hope is that the next wave of women academics and practitioners — those with empathy, creativity, and data acumen — will explore this topic so that companies can continue enthusiastically pursuing their data value creation journeys. In the meantime, I have slightly changed my teaching message: you need to be creating value from your data … in acceptable ways!

Dr. Barbara Wixom is a principal research scientist at the MIT Center for Information Systems Research (CISR). Her research explores how companies generate value from their data assets. Barbara runs a data research advisory board composed of 100 chief data officers from CISR sponsor companies who inform and participate in her research. She has published in top practice and academic journals, including MIT Sloan Management Review, MIS Quarterly Executive, MIS Quarterly, and Information Systems Research, and she regularly presents her work to a diverse array of audiences around the globe. Barbara has been honored for her teaching, case writing, and contributions to the decision support community.

Kathryn Bradley
Strategic Marketing Manager
Postali

Climbing the Ladder Without Losing Yourself

For as long as I can remember, I've been a hard worker. A real type A, over-achieving, competitive individual. I've always admired corporate executives who worked their way to C-suite status and the creative entrepreneurs who grew a successful company from scratch (all while raising kids and doing charity work, of course). Altruistic and accomplished.

But what does "accomplished" even mean? I used to think the answer was universal: owning a house, getting married, making a six-figure salary — the typical indicators of success in our society. But when I asked one of my best friends many years back what she thought being successful was, her answer astounded me: "To me, being successful means that I have grown as a person and am continuing to work on myself and how I treat others. It means I'm happy with where I'm at in life."

Wow. Was it possible for me to feel accomplished in this way, where I was happy without having a sole focus on achieving professional success? I wanted to find out.

My Life Before That Revelation

Every year when I was very young, I would fly solo to Austin, Texas, to visit my dad in the summers. I have fond memories of those trips. I always felt so grown up navigating the airports alone and sitting next to business travelers in their fancy suits — with their laptops and expensive briefcases — off to important meetings and leading a super-exciting life, I imagined. I often fantasized about one day having a similar, successful career.

Growing up, I was one of the weirdos who actually enjoyed school — finishing homework and studying for tests before having fun. I was told good grades would get me into a "good" college, which would then enable me to get a "good" job — much like most Millennials were taught.

In college, I worked even harder, juggling extracurriculars with a part-time job and eventually a couple of unpaid internships. If I could build my references and experience now, getting a job after graduation would be easy, I told myself. However, graduating into a recession made it nearly impossible to find a real job, so I ended up working two to three part-time jobs in the bar industry to pay bills. It was one of the most depressing seasons in my life. Feeling hopeless after getting countless job rejections, I pushed off repayment of my student loans and began to question my self-worth.

Still, I worked hard at the bar and got a side gig helping the sales team promote alcoholic beverages at high-profile events, which is where I was finally able to network and make important connections that would help kickstart my career. I'll never forget a woman who built her own company with nothing but the $20K she had stashed away after two years of collecting tips. She gave me great advice and told me it was OK to "keep my options open" when it came to potential job opportunities. And that's just what I did.

Getting on the Fast Track

I quit my part-time jobs and applied to project management roles because I was good at planning and keeping track of details. I landed my first full-time job with benefits — for a whopping $35K/year! Just like always, I worked my tail off. My manager and the director were both workaholics, and the "culture" they promoted in my interview was basically a "eat lunch at your desk and always be on call" environment. I worked nights, weekends, and holidays. I remember sneaking upstairs to take a call and respond to "a few emails" on the night of my engagement party — and didn't realize how sad and wrong this was until a few days later, when I broke down in the women's restroom at the office. That prompted me to get up the nerve to talk to my manager, who expressed empathy but didn't do anything to help. I knew I

8

needed to make a career change. Expecting to have better luck in my home-town where I had more connections, I applied to jobs out of state. I ended up accepting a position at a marketing agency to "put my communications degree to use," even though the pay was the same as my previous position. The job wasn't perfect, but the culture was a massive improvement. I had a supportive environment with smart co-workers my age and a diplomatic manager who didn't micromanage. The work was constant and fast-paced, which was exciting at first but slowly started to lead to burnout.

Since I felt valued and challenged to take on more work, I was eventually back to working long days (and some weekends). This did help earn me a promotion after two years, where I was given a minor raise. However, I quickly took on even more responsibility, which encouraged me to ask for my first real raise (20%). I came to the table prepared with an unquestionable case, and I ended up getting the pay hike. After four years, my ending salary was double that of my starting one, and I felt untouchable.

The highlight of my time there was when I was offered to fly across the country to meet a VIP client in order to execute their annual review with top mem-bers of our sales team. I spent around 40 hours preparing the presentation, gathering and analyzing years of data, and making sure the sales team was aligned. I was ecstatic for the opportunity but scared shitless at the same time. I knew I needed to look my best, so I splurged on a manicure, new heels, and a blowout the night before. I wore my best professional dress and carried my suitcase in one hand and my laptop bag in the other, as I would be meeting clients later.

As I stood in the TSA line, it hit me: I realized that at the age of 29, I had made my dreams of success come true. I was finally the accomplished business traveler I had aspired to be as a little girl! What a surreal moment — feel-ing on top of the world and proud of myself, yet sad that this is what I had worked a lifetime to achieve. I was at my peak; there was no more money I could make in my role, nowhere else to climb, and I finally understood the saying, "It's lonely at the top."

Getting Back Off the Track

Although I was proud of my success, I knew there was more to life than working 50+ hours a week for the last six years just to reach this moment. I did a lot of self-reflection following that trip, vowing to reprioritize my life. I thought about how, whenever a new contact asked me what I do, my instinct was to share my job title, as if that told them everything they needed to know. My identity had become so wrapped up in my career that I had been neglecting what actually made me happy. I was at the point where I no longer enjoyed the work I was doing; I was busy, but it was mindless.

Within the last year, however, I became increasingly interested in marketing analytics. I paid to attend several conferences, learning as much as I could about the field and eventually meeting a recruiter who helped me get a position as an analyst for a Fortune 500 company. While I worked hard to adjust to a new role, I was no longer client-facing, which gave me breathing room to see things from a new perspective.

Unfortunately, I also witnessed negative attitudes and selfish behaviors in co-workers and managers. I could tell they were already six rungs into their climb up the ladder, and they couldn't (or wouldn't) see the casualties they'd left behind them. I recognized some of this from the way I used to behave, but it was embarrassing to see how far some of these people would go. They didn't hesitate to bark orders at those lower in rank, shame someone publicly, or throw another colleague under the bus, all in vain hopes of shining slightly brighter.

I ended up leaving that company, despite the salary and prestige. I no longer wanted the corporate-climb environment, and I couldn't be more grateful for how I shifted gears in my life — both on and off the clock.

I now know that I want more out of life and that self-improvement is a never-ending process. I also know I can still be the person I have always been — driven, independent, and curious — in a work environment that respects my ideas and values what I bring to the table. So can you.

Find out what your core values and soft skills are and don't be afraid to bring them to work. These are likely to help you succeed in any position and help you stay true to yourself. That way, whether you are looking to climb up, down, or sideways, you won't get lost along the way.

Kathryn Bradley is strategic marketing manager at Postali. She lives in Columbus, Ohio, and enjoys concerts, craft beer, reading, hiking, kayaking, writing, and travel. Kathryn is always up for learning new things, volunteering, meeting new people, and checking out new restaurants and breweries.

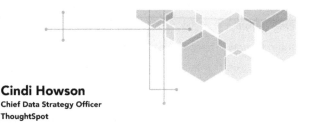

Cindi Howson
Chief Data Strategy Officer
ThoughtSpot

Firsts and The Road Less Traveled

"Two roads diverged in a wood, and I —
I took the one less traveled by,
And that has made all the difference."
Robert Frost

I think about firsts in our careers and in our lives, the moments and memories of joy and accomplishment. My boss gave me a silver dollar as a milestone for the first 100 business intelligence users we onboarded in 1994. It felt as momentous as my first medal in a championship swim meet when I was eight years old. We got a silver dollar for each subsequent set of 100 users, and while I lost my swim medals at some point in growing up, I have cherished these silver dollars for 26 years now.

Why did some firsts pay off and others fail? I think back on three decades of firsts and taking the road less traveled.

A First Global Data Warehouse and BI Deployment
I had been dabbling in various technology and data roles at Dow Chemical, Switzerland, when I was offered the chance to work on the then new data warehousing project: the shared data network (SDN). At first, I said no. The project was being run out of IT, whereas the prior five years I had mainly worked in the business. Some of the European business units did not believe in this project, and there had already been a fair bit of fighting about it.

Ultimately, it was my business VPs — Eddie, Bob, and Fernand — who convinced me to take this project on. These people remain in my mind as visionaries who were always looking for the latest ways technology could help drive the business. We even went so far as installing our own local area network, Novell, before the rest of the company was ready for LANs. IT thought we were nuts to install servers and cables on our own. To this day, my knowledge of routers has served me well, my knowledge of SQL even better.

My indoctrination into the global data warehouse project in 1993 was a single, blue linen–covered book: Bill Inmon's *Building the Data Warehouse*. It was the only resource on the market at that time. Frankly, Ralph Kimball's later work made more sense to me than Inmon's. There were moments in the early days of the SDN project when I just felt like I could not do it. My journal entries from that time are filled with self-doubt, pep talks, and regret. I felt grossly underqualified. Then I'd think, "If not me, then who?" Everything about which BI tool to choose, which security model to use, and who should own which responsibilities was uncharted. My internal voice of self-doubt was already loud enough and further compounded by naysayers both within and outside the project.

A First
The SDN and BusinessObjects deployment launched in 1994, with over 2,000 users globally in the first year. It stood the test of time and laid the foundation for the next 20 years. It was the world's first global data warehouse and the industry's first million-dollar BI deal.

The Lessons Learned
We stayed solely focused on the business users and value delivered. Bleeding-edge technology was merely the vehicle. I wonder how we dared to do what we did, breaking so many entrenched processes. It's only now I wonder whether the diversity of the team — by function, gender, culture, and world region — contributed to our success.

Back to School
The year was 1997, my daughter had just turned one, and I was working part-time at Dow Chemical in Freeport, Texas, as a BI subject matter expert. The role was not as thrilling as the global BI standards leader role I had held

in Switzerland. I can debate whether I was in a less fulfilling role because I had moved countries, because I had returned to work part-time, or because power and politics had come into play. After all, my champions remained in the business units, not in IT, and most of IT had just been outsourced to Andersen Consulting. Regardless of the cause, with a nine-hour workday and a 90-minute commute from Houston to Freeport, I pretty much did not see my daughter three days a week. I was making a sacrifice as a mother for work that was not particularly fulfilling. I had to ask myself: was it even worth it?

Ultimately, I decided it was not. The decision to leave Dow felt like a divorce. I was leaving a family, a team that accomplished the impossible, and even the place where I had met my husband, now of 26 years. How could I possibly leave?

Scarier still, not only did I decide to leave Dow, I decided to go back and get my MBA that year. No salary. No career. All while learning to be a first -time mother. Gulp! The only person more anxious about this decision was my husband. Financially, he thought it was irresponsible. We had only been married three years, and he hadn't yet learned about my lean years in college, when I worked two and three jobs to stay in school. (Now, I call him "the Cindi whisperer.")

I presented my case from every angle: I would have more time at home! More flexibility! An MBA would allow me to earn more money … er, eventually! Maybe? Hopefully?

I had one day to prepare for the GMAT and apply for the fall semester at Houston-area MBA programs. I still consider it a stroke of luck that I landed at Rice, a school I had never even heard of until I discussed my plan with our new friends, the Glasscocks. They told me the MBA program there had a new dean and was going places.

As fate would have it, as soon as I resigned from Dow and accepted my offer at Rice, I learned we were pregnant with our second child. Oops! It felt like a sign from the universe that I should not be going back to school. I looked at the calendar and said to my husband, "Don't worry; the due date is during spring break."

So Many Firsts

All right. This time was nuts. Totally nuts. The baby's due date did not fall quite when we expected. My professors had to trust that I really would take my exam at home, without cheating and while sticking to a 90-minute time limit. I vaguely remember a neighbor proctoring for me. I wrote two pivotal papers in that time, one on work-life balance and the other on how the internet would revolutionize the business intelligence industry. It is this second paper that brought me back to the BI industry with a renewed clarity of purpose on where my combined technical and business talents would have the most impact.

Lessons Learned

Education is the best investment you can ever give yourself. It's not the degree or the certificate. My career would not have evolved the way it did without the knowledge and skills I gained at Rice.

Measures of Success

"Measures of Success" is a chapter in one of my books, *Successful Business Intelligence: Secrets to Unlocking the Value of BI and Big Data*. It is one of six books I have written over the last 17 years.

As I sit here in 2020, with a pandemic, protests, and a fragile world economy, I think about what matters most in work and in life. Can we ever separate the two? How will I measure my own success? Is it by the number of books I have written? My favorite keynote? The roles I have held? Or is it the privilege of joining the C-suite for ThoughtSpot, a company that has disrupted the market and represents the next generation of analytics and BI?

It is none of these things. Instead, I find myself thinking about the people I have been blessed to work with and to have met, sometimes only briefly, and yet who have changed my thinking or inspired me in a single encounter.

I find myself thinking, did I do the same for them? Or did I let my age-old fears and self-doubt silence me in precisely the wrong moment? My path to this life and this work has never been linear. At the risk of sharing too much, my mother lost custody of me when I was 11, and my father largely checked out of my life when I was 18, more permanently at 23. My role models in life and in work have been mixed, and at times, I wonder how and why my spirit has not been broken.

I think about the kindness of people. I wonder, did I get my work-life balance right enough for my children? As I watch them, in their twenties now, both navigate their own losses and disappointments in this pandemic year, I see that when they get knocked down, they work a problem from every angle and get back up again.

My hope is that my example of resilience and hope, despite the odds, will be the gift I have given just one other person in our industry, someone with fewer advantages in life and in education who has had a bigger hill to climb.

Which First?
Will this person be the first woman, the first minority to make it to college in their family? Or will it be the first CDO to disrupt their organization in ways that others have tried and failed at before? Time will tell.

Lessons Learned
Dream big. Imagine the impossible and think outside the box. Don't let anyone else tell you "you can't." Recognize they are merely projecting their own fears and trying to shield you from disappointment. Our own internal voices are sometimes the harshest critics. We have to be kinder to ourselves. I am still learning this lesson.

Cindi is an analytics and BI thought leader and expert with a flair for bridging business needs with technology. As chief data strategy officer at ThoughtSpot, she advises top clients on data strategy and best practices for becoming data-driven, influences ThoughtSpot's product strategy, and is the host of The Data Chief podcast. Cindi was previously a Gartner research vice president, was the lead author for the data and analytics maturity model and analytics and BI Magic Quadrant, and is a popular keynote speaker. She introduced new research in data and AI for good, NLP/BI Search, and augmented analytics and brought both the BI bake-offs and innovation panels to Gartner globally. She's rated a top 12 influencer in big data and analytics by Onalytca, Solutions Review, and Humans of Data. Prior to joining Gartner, Cindi was founder of BI Scorecard, a resource for in-depth product reviews based on exclusive hands-on testing; a contributor to InformationWeek; *and the author of several books, including:* Successful Business Intelligence: Unlock the Value of BI & Big Data *and* SAP BusinessObjects BI 4.0: The Complete Reference. *She served as The Data Warehousing Institute (TDWI) faculty member for more than a decade. Prior to founding BI Scorecard, Cindi was a manager at Deloitte & Touche and a global BI standards leader for Dow Chemical. She has an MBA from Rice University.*

Angelica Bruhnke
CEO
Versatile MED Analytics

From Fantasy to Beyond Blessed: How I Beat the Odds

My childhood dreams consisted of things that seemed more likely obtained from a genie in a bottle than anything that could remotely be within my own grasp. On my father's side, I was a first-generation American from a Mexican family. I grew up poor, experiencing the dysfunction that plagues many impoverished families: alcoholism, domestic violence, hunger. You name it, I experienced it.

In response, I developed a keen interest in fantasy. Whether it be through books or TV, I escaped my reality through fiction. This served me well as a child, allowing me to very easily disconnect from my environment and escape into something better. I dreamed of things like winning lottery tickets or other fortuitous strokes of luck that could change my and my family's life circumstances forever.

As luck would have it, those dreams never came true. Instead, I created my own "luck" by pursuing endeavors well beyond my comfort zone. This wasn't, however, until after I first went down the path of fulfilling a societal stereotype of the poor, Hispanic female. At 15, I was pregnant and well on my way to dropping out of school and continuing the cycle of poverty that was expected of any pregnant teenager. The only thing that stopped that descent was my ability to dream. My ability to dream of a life for my child that was a hundred times better than my own is what kept me from dropping out of school. It's what got me to my high school graduation day as valedictorian and eventually to attaining a master's degree in analytics and pursuing a career that got me to where I am now, CEO of a healthcare analytics company.

Falling in Love with Data

Over the years I developed a love and respect for data, something that had power to change the world — or so I believed, and still believe. After college, where I earned my undergraduate degree in finance, I ended up working in roles that involved sifting through and making sense of large volumes of data. Then I had the fortune of landing in healthcare. Government budget cuts led to the closing of the CPA firm I worked for, and my ensuing career pursuits placed me in a job with Blue Cross Blue Shield. This is where I learned that data could be truly impactful. This is where I found my place in healthcare.

I learned how to program, not something many women did at the time. Programming was a male-dominated field where I didn't have experienced females to look up to, to mentor and guide me. Keep in mind, STEM wasn't a thing when I was growing up, and programming was a field I knew nothing about.

Truth be told, I was drawn to programming because I loved the linguistics of it all. When you really think about it, programming is all about learning a language that allows you to speak to machines. There are multiple languages that exist, depending on the programming application you're using, but the challenge remains the same — you have to speak the right language to make your machine do what you want.

I became enthralled with the ability to "speak" a language that most couldn't. I loved the challenge of troubleshooting communication breakdowns that inevitably occurred when my ask of my machine wasn't communicated in a way that it understood.

I dove into a world of technical complexity I never envisioned. In this adventure, I found my niche. I was able to satisfy both an intellectual thirst — I was constantly learning — and a human need to help make the world a better place by producing actionable data. As clichéd as it sounds, I found my calling. I found what I felt I was meant for. I reached that moment where I was no longer doing a job; I was pursuing a career.

Anyone who works in data and can relate to this feeling knows how wonderful the sentiment is. I found my passion and wanted to learn more. I became … a data wonk. My data pursuits led me to more and more lessons, such as how to take all data with a grain of salt. It was a valuable lesson, taught to me by mentors who showed me how data can easily be misrepresented. It highlighted the art that goes into crafting a data story.

During my time at Blue Cross Blue Shield, I not only gained valuable mentors, but I also met someone who would become my best friend and business partner, Stefany Goradia. Our friendship began when we were troubleshooting code, but eventually we became thick as thieves and bonded over shared frustrations around how powerful data could be if only the healthcare industry were better at using it.

Taking the Next Step

After a decade in healthcare analytics, working for various types of healthcare organizations, I decided there was a new chapter in life I had to explore. I needed to take analytics to the masses and give healthcare the opportunity to interact with data in ways it never had before. In 2017, I quit my full-time job to start a company that would do just that. In the process, I also convinced Stefany to join me.

Despite my logical and risk-averse nature, I took a leap that most analysts would think unfathomable. I hedged my bets on an opportunity where the data showed I was statistically likely to fail. I didn't care, though. I was too convinced that healthcare needed the type of data insights we had to offer and that my gamble would sooner or later work out. As luck — or perseverance — would have it, it did.

Three years later, I am leading a company that is bringing a level of insight to healthcare leaders of all organization types that I could only have dreamed of. With clients in states across the country that are changing how they provide services to members and patients, we are succeeding in fulfilling our mission to change how the world sees and interacts with data to create a better health system and a better society. Each day I have the privilege of living a life that defies the odds. I'm grateful for the blessings I've received and for the strength I had to pursue my dreams. I hope my story inspires you to do the same.

Angelica Bruhnke is the CEO of Versatile MED Analytics, a fast-growing healthcare analytics company created with the mission to change how the world sees and interacts with data to create a better health system and a better society.

Angelica has a passion for putting actionable analytics into the hands of healthcare leaders to drive clinical and financial improvements. Drawing on her education and experience in finance and advanced analytic tools, principles, and methodologies, Angelica provides analytic strategy to enable clients to become data-driven organizations. Over the last 14 years, she has brought a diverse perspective to various senior positions held with large healthcare organizations. Her responsibilities across these organizations have included providing data-driven opportunity identification and recommendations for implementing data-driven clinical and operational initiatives, implementing benchmarking used to gauge organizational performance, developing self-service programmatic solutions to manual processes, and training users on utilizing enterprise-wide technical solutions.

Angelica holds an MS in analytics with a concentration in healthcare from Dakota State University and a BBA with a concentration in finance from the University of New Mexico.

When she isn't working, Angelica is a horror aficionado and Chicago Bears fanatic and enjoys reading, writing, spending time with her human/canine family, and test-driving new recipes in her kitchen.

Kiran Mayee Nabigaru
Senior Business Intelligence Developer
Progressive Insurance

Conquering the Fear of Failure

*"Think like a queen. A queen is not afraid to fail.
Failure is another stepping-stone to greatness."*
Oprah Winfrey

Being a woman born and raised in a country where we are stereotyped as less successful, less competitive, less confident, weak, not assertive enough to lead, and many other adjectives, I wasn't taught how to be fearless and face failure with courage. One thing I realized as I got older was that I simply avoided things I wasn't good at. I was always scared of facing potential failure, which kept me away from learning things.

As time passed, I began to experience failure, and I learned that the more I failed, the better my successes became. I began to embrace my failures rather than avoiding them. Here's a story of one of my failures as a BI developer at my former company.

Falling Down

A few years ago, I was working for an e-commerce solutions company when our team was introduced to a new tool to create data visualizations and analyze the data to make data-driven decisions. I was tasked with creating an inventory analysis dashboard to understand the statistics around our company's warehouse actions. As it was my first data visualization project, I was excited to work on it and deliver it successfully on time.

My manager was the only person on our team who had expertise creating visualizations using that tool, so she would usually review the dashboards to ensure the data quality before publishing them to the production server. Because she was supposed to leave early that day for vacation, however, she didn't have time to review my dashboard. Knowing that I always do an in-depth data evaluation and impact analysis before delivering any project, she trusted me to deploy it to production without any further assessment.

When I opened Outlook the next morning, there were several emails about load failures that impacted all the important KPI dashboards that were supposed to be updated by early morning. There was an error in the data source extract due to various code changes I made for the dashboard I was working on. The entire team had to spend a significant amount of time figuring out exactly what the error was and how to fix it, as everybody on the team had limited experience working with that tool. My manager was informed of the failure, and even though she was on vacation, she logged in to fix the issue. It was an epic failure on my part, as I had neglected to do proper impact analysis, causing inconvenience to all our customers and costing the entire team valuable time and effort.

Getting a Hand Up

I was devastated and upset that I failed to meet my manager's expectations and broke her trust. I feared what her reaction would be for the mess I created. The day she returned to work, I went to her and took accountability for the error I made and assured her that I would do thorough testing and impact analysis going forward.

I still remember the exact words she spoke to me on that day. She said, "Fail fast, and fail often. The sooner you can admit failure and walk away from it, the faster you can focus on your next success. Allow a certain amount of time to wallow. Once that time is up, work on it. We are humans; we are not perfect. We do make mistakes, but what is more important is how we turn our mistakes into opportunities to learn and develop."

She shared how losing has helped her to win at things that she thought she would never have achieved in her personal and professional lives. Her stories and experiences restored my self-confidence and inspired me to do better at work and in my life. I am so grateful that I got an opportunity to work with an amazing woman who always inspires, motivates, and encourages other women to achieve their goals.

Two Critical Qualities

Two important qualities of mine that rebuilt my boss's trust in me even after my failure are accountability and credibility. Being accountable for our actions is one of the most vital qualities we can possess. People who take accountability seriously are self-aware of the outcomes of their actions.

Credibility is no less important. I learned about the concept of a "credibility bank" in Carrie Kerpen's book *Work It: Secrets for Success from the Boldest Women in Business*. In the book, she discusses how each one of us has the ability to build our own credibility bank. It is our responsibility to take steps on a regular basis to fill up the bank, as we never know when it will save us during a failure.

When I started as an intern at the e-commerce company, my credibility bank was zero, as I hadn't done anything yet. Nobody knew what I was capable of. It was my hard work, dedication, and focus that helped me to gain trust and credibility from my team. I had already completed three years of working for that company when I made the dashboard project error, so my credibility bank was full by that time, as I'd done a lot of great work throughout my tenure.

When I failed to deliver my first project, I thought my credibility was completely lost and that I wouldn't be assigned any other key projects going forward. To my surprise, my manager reached out to me to lead a much bigger project. That's when I realized that our credibility may be damaged temporarily, but it can never be lost completely. It is this credibility that landed me another project even after I failed at delivering my first one successfully.

Always remember that failures are stepping-stones to success. Never ever shy away from failing because it's through failures that we learn the greatest lessons that life can teach us. We live in a world where failures feel like the end of our journey, but that is not the case. Many success stories start with a failure story. In fact, the most successful people in the world have failed multiple times until they achieve success. It is imperative to teach girls at an early age how to both conquer the fear of failure and bounce back harder to achieve their goals.

Kiran Mayee Nabigaru is an idealistic, goal-oriented, and career-driven individual who strongly believes that anything in life is achievable if we can turn our mistakes into lessons and fears into courage.

Kiran received an MS in business intelligence/analytics from Nova Southeastern University. She is currently working as a senior BI developer for Progressive Insurance.

In her time away from work, Kiran enjoys blogging about fitness and lifestyle. She inspires many young girls to follow a healthy lifestyle by sharing her workout routines and healthy cooking recipes on her social media blog page.

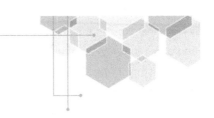

Emma Dietz
Product Manager
Progressive Insurance

Not Knowing Everything Might Make You Better at Your Job

Some people worry they will be looked down upon if they do not know the answer to a question. Others fear they won't be able to progress in their career because they lack the "right" answer for every situation. Many people believe the managers and directors above them got to the levels they did because they knew what to do in every scenario. That may be true on the margins, but it's the exception, not the rule.

It shouldn't be a secret: you don't need to have all the answers to be good at your job. However, you must know when to admit you don't know (even if only to yourself), and you must be willing to put in the time and energy to find the people who do have the answers you need.

Ask and You Shall Receive (the Answers You Need)
I started at Progressive straight out of college with a BA in economics — probably one of the last graduating classes that didn't really use Excel beyond the analysis required for that final senior project. My new job required me to use Excel for just about every minute of my day, which was a big learning curve. I spent a lot of time sticking my head out of my cubicle to snag the attention of my more tenured analyst colleagues: "Hey, can you help me with…?" "Do you have a minute to explain…?" As a new hire, I found that those words left my mouth more often than I cared to admit those first months.

Eventually I stopped asking so many questions, and after a year, I moved from that role to one in another department. In the new position, I also had to ask a lot of questions at the beginning. But again, as before, I stopped asking for help or opinions after a few months. I believed I was fine, that I knew enough and was learning and developing toward the next level.

And then I didn't get promoted. That was the wake-up call that sticks with me over a decade later.

I might have (embarrassingly) become a little upset at that performance review. Looking back, I'm not sure exactly why I had expected to be promoted. No one had given me that impression, except that I had received solid feedback on some recent projects. My manager was a wonderful woman who took my tears in stride. Later, once I was able to think more clearly (and with a little less self-pity), I promised myself to learn as much as I could in order to get that next promotion.

It was difficult for me. I tended to get absorbed into projects, and as an introvert, I had a habit of plugging away at my desk with little interaction with others. I assumed my co-workers probably were too busy to help me — after all, they weren't chatting away; they were working as hard as I was! However, I reasoned with myself, if I didn't know the answer, and I wanted to produce better and more thoughtful results, then I had to ask my peers for their thoughts: "Have you ever run into this problem before?" "What am I missing?" "Can I walk you through this analysis?" I found myself outside my cubicle more often, talking to others in the halls and breakroom, via emails and over the phone. I found I was learning more and faster than I had been before, and I also was producing better work.

My previous assumption had been wrong: my co-workers were actually happy to help! I only had to ask. Even so, to avoid being "a pest," I tried to ensure I had some idea of what I was talking about before checking in with a contact, and I endeavored to keep my questions brief. If necessary, I would ask the same questions of several co-workers before I felt I had learned enough to move on. Getting help, opinions, and advice from my peers enabled me to produce better work and greatly expanded my network at the company.

The Benefits of Becoming a Sponge

Not long after that awkward performance review, I chose to move to another business area. This time, I was working for a manager who had an intimidating amount of experience at our company and in previous roles at startups in other industries. Nevertheless, I maintained my resolution to ask questions and learn as much as I could: I was a sponge.

My new manager did not seem to mind answering questions. He was, in fact, great at explaining things. I learned how to solve common business problems (and a few not-so-common ones). I learned how to influence others and lead projects. I learned enough to get promoted, not once but twice in the four years I spent as an analyst on that team.

Then a job opening came up — a management role that would make me (more or less) a peer of my current manager. I felt ready and energized about the position. After a grueling set of interviews, describing all the leading, influencing, and problem-solving I had done to date in my career, I got the job. I was so excited and proud!

That job transition was very stressful. As a manager or project leader, you make the decisions. Often an analyst or someone with data expertise builds the queries, designs the spreadsheets, and runs the models, and you are expected to use that information to develop the answer to the problem at hand — an answer that sometimes makes its way up to the division president or even to the CFO or CEO. (No pressure!)

This was terrifying. Despite my analytical background, I felt completely unprepared for a job that I believed expected me to know everything. No one really told me you don't have to magically know the answer. Fortunately, I reverted to my new-old habits (asking questions and being a sponge), and I was able to come up with answers. Things got easier, and I learned to thrive in the new role.

The Secrets to Continuous Learning

As I write this essay seven years later (now with a team of my own to manage), I see four key things that enable a person to continuously learn and produce high-quality results, which often advances one's career. You must be willing to:

1. Say "I don't know."

Don't stop there, though. Follow it with, "But I can find out." This demonstrates that you're a team player and willing to tackle big problems (because if the answer were obvious, it wouldn't be a "big" problem). It's OK to admit when you don't know something; no one likes a know-it-all.

2. Put in the work to find the answer.

In a big organization, it may take many false starts to identify the person with the answer, and it may not just be a single person who has what you need. Be prepared for your search to develop over many emails, phone calls, and meetings. Whether or not you find the right person or group (and hopefully you will), your network of contacts will have grown. This will help you tackle the next problem that comes along.

3. Ask the unasked question.

Give yourself some credit: if you have a question during a meeting or conversation, nine times out of 10, someone else has the same one. Don't be afraid to ask — you're helping others learn (and clearing up your own confusion too).

4. Be willing to listen to the answer.

Sometimes the answer may contradict what (you think) you know. Use your network and learn as much as you can so you can find an answer that satisfies everyone involved.

None of these things is guaranteed to get you that next job or promotion, but the literature is clear that good leaders are often collaborative, and diversity of thought helps produce excellent business results. Using these four tactics can certainly go a long way toward helping you achieve a solid, productive career at any level.

Emma Dietz began her professional career in 2006 after graduating from Carleton College with a BA in economics. She started at Progressive Insurance as an entry-level analyst and has held several positions since then, working her way up to a product manager position. Emma is currently responsible for the P&L of a top 10 state in Progressive's auto division. She also manages a small team of analysts and enjoys helping them advance their own careers. Outside of work, she enjoys spending time with her husband and young daughter, traveling (when safe to do so), and reading.

Shereen Mosallam
Leader
Symbios Solutions

From 0 to Hero: My Story, An Inspiration

Having just graduated from university, I happily accepted my bachelor's degree in mechanical engineering, which shone with the bright future I had at hand. With ambition in my heart and strength in my gut, I knew I wanted to do something substantial with the knowledge I recently acquired. From the very beginning, I wanted to explore a career as an engineer at General Motors, my justified intent when I began a job there. My journey then took me to the American University in Cairo, where I was a statistics professor, before I was headhunted to become a consulting entrepreneur in Six Sigma in 2005. However, my story begins with the misogynistic patriarchy of Egyptian sexism showing its demeaning face as soon as I began to explore the work field.

Making My Way Despite Resistance

I realized in my freshman year of college that I was at a disadvantage. As the only girl in my class of 1993 who was studying mechanical engineering, I was set up for failure from day one. I was told I would not graduate to a fulfilling career, as companies would prefer men to work in the field. However, this only made me work harder to achieve my goals, fueling me to excel in everything I did. While all my female classmates chose to pursue the generally more "girl-dominated" majors, such as psychology, nursing, and architecture, I decided to take on mechanical engineering. I believed that being a woman would give me insight on the field that others would not have.

Unfortunately, GM's manufacturing team did not see it that way when I first applied for their summer training internship in 1993. Thankfully, discrimination is prohibited at General Motors, so they ultimately accepted me after seeing that my qualifications matched — and in some cases exceeded — those of the other candidates who applied. Nevertheless, I was reluctantly accepted as a female trainee working with operators on production lines. I went on to become the first female engineer in the company, where I was proud to work in quality control.

Working in quality control was an interesting experience. Not only was I charged with ensuring the success of our current projects, I was also responsible for brainstorming ways to better them. My team and I would work countless hours to develop new ways to sell, produce, and market the products. However, something was off. I realized that the tactics used to brainstorm new ideas were inefficient. I quickly figured out the reason for this was that people would not use the actual data from our previous production and quality record to form solutions based on it. Instead, they would create unnecessary changes that did not enhance the product. This was the first time I ever detected a problem in the actual management process instead of the machine.

In one instance, the device that raises and lowers the glass windows for trucks was having a lot of mechanical problems that led to product failure in the market, which GM's people were unable to solve. My colleagues focused more on the mechanical aspects of the device instead of analyzing the data to figure out which aspect of it was failing. My endless cries to look through the data were ignored, so I decided to take on the task myself and led a personal data-driven analysis. Once I discovered that the problem lay not in the technical aspects of the device but more in the installation of it, I took my findings to the manufacturing, engineering, marketing, and after-sales departments, where I was praised. The happiness in my chest once I solved the problem was undeniable, and I believe that this is when I truly found my calling.

Pursuing — and Sharing — Knowledge

The high of finding the solution that others could not quickly turned into a consuming need for knowledge. I felt like I needed to learn more about data processing in order to excel at both my job at GM and in my overall career, so I signed up for several advanced statistics courses. I decided to leave General Motors in 2000 and move on to work on Six Sigma, a set of techniques that are used for process improvement. While Six Sigma is central to business strategy, I still felt like it was not enough. I believed there was more data that companies could be using but were unable to due to their lack of knowledge on how to apply the data to tools. I came to the conclusion that companies do not efficiently utilize statistics in technical aspects, which leads to a lack of data-driven decision-making.

Knowing this, I decided to expand my knowledge of statistics by taking a U.K.-based Six Sigma Master Black Belt Certification course. Understanding the intricacies of Six Sigma made me a prime candidate to be headhunted by Symbios Consulting as a consultant in 2005. Since then, I have been working for Symbios as a Master Black Belt and leading Middle East Lean, Six Sigma, and supply chain teams to deploy Lean supply chain and Six Sigma efforts in Egyptian and Middle East organizations. I have delivered training and led deployments in several countries, including the U.K., U.S., United Arab Emirates, Jordan, South Africa, Saudi Arabia, Morocco, Egypt, and Romania.

In 2017, I took analytics courses and learned computer analytics to almost an expert degree. I soon understood how much people could use computing power to automate analysis. This elated me, as I had dedicated the past three years of my life to learning analytics and teaching statistics. The combination of my knowledge of analytics and operations excellence made me a highly valued individual in the field.

I invested my intelligence in the field of analytics into a Six Sigma course, a course I both developed and taught, by adding a data analytics module to the Six Sigma Black Belt Program. I also created a separate certification called the Data Analytics Practitioner Program. The goal of this program was to reach those who were more in the business sector, not software engineers such as myself. The program taught students how to use ready-made packages such as Microsoft Azure ML, a machine learning software solution, in order to enhance data science knowledge.

I began to take data science courses in order to learn how to work with both data science and people in order to use data to the highest degree in all aspects of work. This led me to create my first data procedure: the 17-step analytics road map. As a general analogy, I believe data to be the backbone of any automation and digitalization initiative. The success of the road map soon led to the digitalization triangle, a marketing strategy that combines the forces of data analytics, customer journey, and process mining in order to effectively utilize a company's resources and data in real-life applications.

The success of the Data Analytics Practitioner Program inspired me to open my Symbios Digital company, which focuses on digitalization and data excellence, in 2019. With the slogan "From 0 to Hero" in mind, I pursued consulting work with big companies that have a lot of data but not the ability to correctly use it. I have several success stories to my credit, and as of 2020, I can say with the utmost pride that my business has branches in Egypt, Saudi Arabia, U.A.E., and the U.S.

I believe that data talks, but people don't know how to listen to it. I am here to bridge the language gap.

Shereen Mossallam is an experienced Lean Six Sigma Master Black Belt with a demonstrated history of working in the management consulting industry. Shereen is skilled in analytics, process mining, BI, DMAIC, operational excellence, SCOR, Industry 4.0 readiness, digitalization strategy, value stream mapping, Lean deployment, strategy deployment, and manufacturing operations. She is a strong business development professional with an MBA focused on business adminis-tration, management, and operations from the American University in Cairo.

Sravanthi Vallampati
IT Manager
Progressive Insurance Corporation

From Information to Inspiration

11:43 a.m., 2/24/1995. It was a cold, gray day in Dayton, Ohio.

I was 8,328 miles away from certainty: the warmth of family and comfort of home. With one familiar face — that of my husband, whom I had known for 17 days — I stepped out of the airport and into an adventure. Lost, lonely, and limp from two days of travel, I couldn't decide what I wanted to do, yet the next thing I knew, it was 11 p.m., and the refrigerator was empty.

Wow! #1: A meal for two at Taco Bell — $3.96.

Wow! #2: Cub Foods was open 24 hours. As if the stadium-lit ceiling and the unending expanse of aisles were not enough, it offered an eye-popping selection of merchandise I had never seen before.

Wow! #3: In the midnight awe of stepping out to explore as a resident of the United States for the first time, my eyes settled on a label: $1.72. At an exchange rate of rupees 39.2 for $1, a bottle of Revlon nail polish in my favorite shade of plum was less than rupees 100. I asked my husband if I could buy two. With a kind smile, he said, "Of course!"

To truly understand the journey of a 23-year-old new bride on an H-4 visa and appreciate the pain of displacement, the pressure of figuring life out, and the pleasure of small wins, you'd have to peek into my head, beat as my heart, and walk in my path.

Let the Learning Begin

It wasn't long before I realized the only antidote to homesickness was a preoccupation. The ready learner in me not only devoured information, but also worked up a glutton's appetite for it. Scale conversions, furniture and household gadgets assembly, driver's license test, etc. were a breeze. I even wrote a few poems, but my most diligent work was the yellow notebook. For a single-income family with a two-digit checking account buffer at the end of each pay period, tracking was mandatory. The Dollar General became my favorite store, and a hot chocolate with whipped cream, my weekend treat for zero bounced checks. In studying credit card statements and asking questions of them, I made staggering discoveries: fine print, credit limits, terms of payment, no-interest loans, and same-as-cash. *I was digging this stuff!*

For a small hike in pay, we moved to Cleveland a year later. I remained hooked onto dial-up to read technology-related posts in user groups. I reveled in those fuzzy conversations, which I didn't fully understand, but the discomfort of geeking out on complexity was refreshing. Talk of Y2K was catching on like wildfire, and the term information technology, or IT — the place everyone wanted to be but me — finally registered.

I had tethered my dream of becoming a teacher to two bachelor's degrees and a master's degree. I held on to that dream with trepidation. In hindsight, I realize what a sore gap not having an informed mentor or an invested friend is. My husband and I just wanted careers that would help us succeed. While the wannabe teacher in me refused to relent, teaching as a career option no longer felt viable. I was convinced that no one would sponsor my visa and hire me — a non-native speaker of English — to teach the language, so I did not even try. Disappointed but not defeated, my sense of unwarranted optimism kicked into high gear. *Unbeknownst to me, I had switched from ready learner to problem solver.*

My appetite for information and curiosity to look beyond the obvious continued to soar, but not enough to secure me a job in IT. The more I looked around, the less equipped I felt to embark on the digital highway. So I chose to go back to school to get an associate degree in computer information systems in spring 1997. *My motivation to succeed found a fitting match in my wish to write a story that was, let's just say, different.*

As I waited for my H-1B visa, I spent my time acquiring three Microsoft certifications, including Certified Trainer. Who knew my bachelor's in education and master's in English literature would come to my rescue? My first job was at a Microsoft Training and Solution Provider. I was ecstatic!

My mentor, Brett, groomed me with tact and tenderness, until one day, he answered my harmless inquiry for a lightweight assignment by handing me two Seagate Software Crystal Reports Developer's Guides and a link to a shared drive. With much help and trial and error, I automated printing of birth certificates for the Ohio Bureau of Vital Statistics. That ask was the key to opening the door to my evolving tryst with data, analytics, and insight — and to earning my first career success. *Twenty-two years later, I can say, I continue to ask.*

New learning, newer responsibilities, and nuanced ways of thinking, doing, and learning ensued. In the years that followed, I wore one consultant hat after another: reporting analyst, SQL developer, data analyst, data warehouse developer, etc. Consulting exposed me to depth, and my reporting specialist role at a family-owned durable medical equipment distributor gave me breadth. While the struggle to transform information to insight end-to-end with a team of two was real, the reward was multifold invigorating.

Time to Reflect ... and Pivot

Losing my mom in 2000 and my dad four years later, in my eighth month of pregnancy, almost broke me. It forced me to reflect and lean in for help. I stayed home through my maternity leave and for a few months more. I finally had time to slow down. As I recovered, I thought more intentionally about my career, the differences between data, analytics, and insight, and their relevance to my journey thus far. I was enjoying connecting the dots. *I was finally getting IT.*

I joined Progressive Corporation in 2007. Its Fortune 500 scale was awe-inspiring. The Enterprise Reporting and Analytics team of eight felt like home. My manager cared about her team, and her team, its newest teammate. The pace was brisk and the persuasion to work, powerful!

Four months in, I was leading an enterprise migration. Moving 11,934 data/information/decision-making personnel in 42 groups to a new reporting platform seemed an insurmountable challenge. I was introduced to scale, cost-benefit analysis, technical rigor, negotiation, tradeoff fundamentals, and, most notably, customer personas almost overnight.

Change was hard to sell and even harder to manage. I owe my survival to my most able project manager. I'd cry myself to sleep each night yet jump back into the saddle the next morning. There was something sticky about *the voice of the customer — something I could not ignore.* I learned how the impact of IT's priorities wasn't at the program/project level, but at the people level. I worked with the customers, our end users, to address their need to understand, adapt to, and manage the demands of the change we were proposing. Without their agency, change would not happen.

After the fact, I was told my efforts made a difference to how the end users felt: heard and understood. The reward for success was another challenge: this time, it was a migration off a desktop productivity suite. How do I ask the multitudes married to their Excel spreadsheets and Access databases to abandon their loves, and by extension, their bread and butter? While in the garden one morning, it dawned on me that I did not have to sell or tell — just ask and listen. *As simple as it sounded on the surface, it was the very thing we could have been doing better.*

I embraced my aha! moment at the cost of rewriting the approach. My soulful selling led to a technology-agnostic approach to earning customer trust, and while the proposed solution hadn't changed, how we partnered for win-win did. This time, I was proactive in seeking and utilizing the voice of the customer, something I vowed would be my mantra for everything from that day forward!

Continuing to Evolve

In the 2014-2015 marketplace, the promise of data and the impact of analytics continued to become more compelling. Data, big and small, was currency — it was the new gold, oil, superfood, etc. At Progressive, it was our asset. Synergies were unfolding; attitude, architecture, and strategic direction were changing. With senior management buy-in and some extraordinary funding, a new State of Analytics initiative sought to blur the lines between IT and business, to show data the reverence it deserved and use it to bolster our business's vision for the future. *We had work to do, but the momentum was visible, the value was tangible, and our energy was palpable!*

I've learned that if there is an imperative for individuals and corporations alike, it is that they stay open-minded, expect and accept change, and pivot as needed with a can-do spirit and must-do resolve to build something of which they can be truly proud. Today, my former team of eight is a platform of over 100. The ideals we worked toward to build a world-class analytics environment are the norm. Data is cleaner and freer, information is more accurate and timelier, and insight is more within reach than ever before. *We continue to evolve.*

From a personal development standpoint, the last five years have been empowering. If I brought my A-game forward, there was no limit to what I could experience in a nurturing corporate environment where diversity is welcomed, thought leadership is encouraged, inclusion is intentional, and creativity is rewarded. I am not a natural storyteller, but I feel compelled to retell my stories (beyond data) at my clubs as a Toastmaster, at Progressive's Open Houses as a brand ambassador, at the analyst development programs at Progressive and Case Western University's Weatherhead School of Management as a mentor, to youth in my volunteer endeavors as a coach, and to friends as their wing woman.

I believe we are all exposed to continents of data and information from which we draw insights to lead ourselves to our definitions of success. Yet the differentiator is in how we intentionally deploy our head, heart, and hands in work we enjoy. Work that lets the overwhelm dissipate and meaning emerge. Work that promotes a personal brand worth following.

11:50 a.m. 9/24/2020. It's a gorgeous day in Cleveland, Ohio, with a slight nip in the air, sedums and sunflowers in bloom. It's a perfect moment to dedicate my story to all who believe that leaning in, leveraging our definition of success, and leading with it can transform us into inspired individuals.

A distinguished Toastmaster, Sravanthi Vallampati works as an IT manager at Progressive Insurance. She is a customer-centric and results-informed technologist with over 20 years of experience who harmonizes numbers with stories and delights in the many aha! moments that her work at and outside of Progressive brings. She lives in Aurora, Ohio, with her husband Nalini Mohan and their two daughters, Apoorva and Pooja. Sravanthi says that her success comes from being an inspired, unbroken spirit that revels in creating an inclusive environment of unwarranted optimism and belief that it will endure.

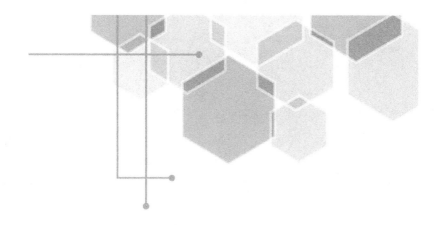

STRATEGY

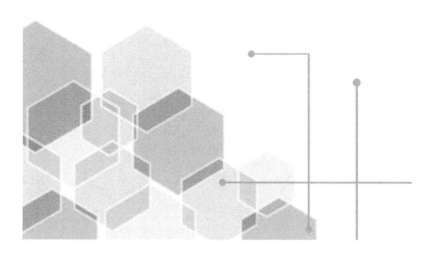

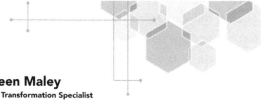

Kathleen Maley
Analytics Transformation Specialist
Maley Analytics Advisory

Bridging the Divide Between Great Analytics and Business Value

If you've ever played Minesweeper, you have felt the elation that comes when you finally know — after countless painful missteps — the answer to one of the best logic puzzles ever created. I love that feeling. I'm addicted to it. It's why I still love analyzing data. These days, I solve different types of problems, but the process is largely the same: identify the problem, gather data, analyze it, develop a hypothesis, fail and adjust, until, all of a sudden, the answer comes into view.

One of the biggest problems facing analytics professionals today is the persistent disconnect between the work we do and the value it should generate. We were told that if we did a few simple (but not easy) things — learn the business, gather context, use "business speak" and never mention p-values, create solutions relevant to business objectives, represent solutions in terms of business opportunity, and gain business buy-in — then our partners would surely leverage our solutions. But even after all of that, companies say they still aren't getting the value they were promised.

So how can we bridge the divide between the great analytics we produce and the business's ability to capitalize on it?

In answering the question above, I'll first tell you about an experience of my own. I'll then share what I learned from it. Finally, I'll provide five recommendations for putting that knowledge into practice.

The $6 Million Opportunity

Not too long ago, I was invited to work with an organization that was struggling to reduce its customer service call volume. The organization had created self-service capabilities to address the issue, but their release had little to no impact on call volume. After thoroughly analyzing customer-profile and cross-channel engagement data, I was able to correct several misconceptions and establish an accurate understanding of who was calling, what actions they were calling to take, and why they were choosing to call instead of self-serve.

Based on this new understanding of the data, primary business objective, and operational constraints, we decided to build a customer-level indicator that would be used to inform a new call-routing strategy. Very conservatively, this initiative had an associated cost savings of $6 million annually — a more than 20-fold return on investment.

Before beginning my analysis, I did all the things I've learned to do. I understood the business and their objectives; I gathered the appropriate context; I put the solution and opportunity in relevant terms. My work was understood, and the potential opportunity represented real money. Leadership, the head of the call center, and the team were thrilled!

But when it came to implementing and adopting the solution, the business was wholly unprepared. It's important to note that the issue wasn't lack of "buy-in" or an inability to execute in the general sense. There was no question that it was my job to build the indicator, but we'd had no discussion about the business change management required to leverage the new indicator. So when it came time to do so, there was no implementation team in place, and the $6 million opportunity was at risk.

My primary objective is to help the business create value through the use of analytics. In the case above, that meant not only producing a relevant analytical solution, but also guiding the business through their own change management. That's when it became clear to me that analysts needed to add one more task to their already long list of duties: they need to help their business partners learn how to be great users of analytical solutions. In fact, I'll go as far as to say it's unrealistic, a bit unfair, and totally unproductive to expect them to just figure it out on their own. Here's a better way:

1. Create and work toward a shared business objective.

This starts with understanding and communicating that there is no such thing as an analytics initiative — only a business initiative. As described in the case above, by not consciously establishing this way of thinking, I inadvertently created a psychological hurdle for myself and my partner. We were focused on the analytical component of the initiative — the indicator — but gave much less energy to our real objective: reducing call volume and creating a $6 million efficiency.

2. Set realistic expectations up front.

It is almost always easier to develop an analytical solution than it is to implement it. If I don't make that clear at the outset, then a couple of things happen. First, my partner will feel duped — like I made a promise to deliver a solution, but now it turns out all I've done is create a bunch of work for them. Fair or unfair, that is how they will feel. Second, if they haven't planned for the initiative, they won't have budgeted for it in person-hours and/or dollars. In this case, even if they want to implement the solution, it might not be possible. This is the worst possible outcome: a good solution can't be leveraged, time and effort have been wasted, and everyone is frustrated.

3. Explain the analytical process.

The fact that different problems require different solutions is a familiar concept for me, but that is often not the case for my business partner. Whether I'm answering an ad hoc question, creating a dashboard, or building a predictive model, there is a certain process I will follow. Walking my partner through the high-level "what" and "why" of my process demystifies the experience and enables better planning on their part. It also gives me the opportunity to explain at the outset what I'll need from them.

4. Ask how the solution will be used.

In addition to asking the business what problem they need to solve, asking how they intend to use the solution has proved to be a useful and non-threatening way to start their change management wheels turning. When I asked this question in the case above, I did so because I knew that the relevance of the indicator was directly tied to its intended use. A secondary, albeit unintentional, benefit was my partner's realization that they hadn't yet thought that through. This question triggered the development of their adoption strategy, the critical component of our eventual success.

5. Participate in business change management planning.

Although business initiatives are typically owned and run by the business that will benefit from them, I still play an important role in the project-planning process. As the analytics expert, I will be aware of opportunities and risks that might not be visible to the business. For example, I know that my development data has to align with data that is available in the system in which the indicator will be implemented. As a result, I need to facilitate a decision on the production platform sooner rather than later. This is also the time to establish the importance of back-end performance monitoring and to include those deliverables — for me and for the business — into the overall project plan.

For the last decade and a half, analytics professionals have been focused on upstream requirements like data quality, relationship building, and understanding business strategy. We have made significant strides in these areas, and our analytical solutions are more reliable, relevant, and sophisticated than ever before. Launching from this strong foundation, we can now turn our energy toward downstream implementation and adoption. Only by filling this last big gap will we finally see our organizations achieve the value we've been promising.

Kathleen Maley is a business leader specializing in the science of data and analytics. She is a cultural change agent in the adoption of analytical strategies and guides business leaders toward better outcomes by integrating data into their business processes. After 15+ years of success through trial and error, her passion is now found in helping organizations leapfrog her early experience to accelerate their journey toward value-generating analytics.

Kathleen started her career on the leading edge of a revolution in data-based decision-making at Bank of America. She built predictive models and led several business analytics verticals. In her culminating role as the bank's consumer deposits pricing executive, she transformed the business from intuition-based to predictive model-based, creating an efficiency of $65 million per basis point saved.

As the head of consumer analytics at KeyBank, Kathleen increased the economic impact of her team by elevating their role from data provider to strategic partner. She established a discipline for measuring realized benefit of analytically informed business initiatives and engineered a shift toward collaboration, ensuring analytical solutions are developed hand in hand with business execution plans.

Kathleen is a board member at the Turner Syndrome Society of the United States, a published writer, and a frequent speaker. She holds degrees in mathematics and applied statistics. Previously, Kathleen taught high school mathematics and statistics in Costa Rica, Mexico, and China. She advises on analytics strategy, offers corporate workshops, and is available for speaking engagements.

Jennifer Heider
Senior Insights Analyst
Huntington Bank

Excellence in Analytics

"We are what we repeatedly do. Excellence, then, is not an act, but a habit."
Will Durant

My first data science project out of college was for a retailer looking for insights into their store traffic, which had declined drastically from previous years. Several teams worked to ingest and prepare individual weekly store traffic files, and then worked to overlay local events and social media analysis to search for potential drivers of store traffic. While we found some patterns, we struggled to identify what might be causing such a sharp decline.

Finally, our chief data scientist asked us to verify the record count in the raw weekly traffic data. It turned out that the earliest years in the dataset contained duplicated weeks that we had not noticed, and once these were removed, the store traffic trend was mostly flat. No matter what fancy method we used to investigate store traffic, no results were going to provide business value until the basic data quality issue was addressed.

No Substitute for Discipline

The internet and most LinkedIn job postings would have you believe that the best data scientists have an impressive mix of software development skills, statistics knowledge, and business acumen and can explain hundreds of algorithms on the spot. It is true that these skills (and others) are important to a successful analytics team and that any wise professional is always looking for new skills to build and ways to innovate. However, the ever-elusive rock star data scientist is just a myth. The best analytics professionals I have worked with have the same core leadership, communication, and organizational skills as the best professionals I have worked with, period.

This is good news for the aspiring data scientist because all it takes is practice and self-discipline — not raw talent — to be methodical, collaborative, and innovative. The best way to learn analytics is by doing the work: ingesting a dataset, writing code to prepare it, and working through error messages as they come.

Professional skills such as organization are particularly useful to data projects. Data science work is undeniably detailed, and it takes discipline to plan and set priorities and check over work to get details correct. Phrases such as "garbage in, garbage out" are typically used to describe models built on data that is incomplete or untrustworthy, but they can be applied to any analytics work. While there are tools to assist with the heavier lifting of ETL and data preparation, additional code is often needed to prepare data for modeling or analysis. An experienced professional may have been doing similar work for years and be able to accomplish these tasks more quickly, but no one is too talented to check the basics: record counts before and after joins, data types, and missing values. Thorough commenting of code and documentation of assumptions, data sources, and data gaps are critical for repeatability and maintainability.

Depending on the maturity of a data science team, quality assurance could vary in formality. Whether QA is done through systematic testing of code in production or ad hoc code sharing with team members, it is important to be disciplined, humble, and willing to ask for help to ensure that the basics are correct. A perfectly tuned neural network built on a faulty dataset is not useful to anyone.

Being accountable, setting reasonable deadlines, checking over work, and validating and documenting assumptions are important steps in an analytics project, but they may get overlooked because they do not make for an exciting conference talk or blog post. Numerous leadership and professional development books have been written that provide advice on how to build these good habits.

Collaboration Is Key

Unless analytics work is being done at a research organization, where learning for learning's sake may be the goal, value is realized when analytics is used for decision-making. Data science adoption relies on a team to, first and foremost, listen to the needs of the business so that the work done addresses the underlying questions and pain points. Throughout the project, the team should partner with the business decision makers and frequently solicit feedback. Finally, results need to be communicated effectively and clearly.

Most companies also have a data team or IT partners that work closely with data scientists and data analysts to manage the data environment and assist with deploying models to production. It is important that these partners be involved in projects early and often to ensure that the end solution is feasible in the desired time frame. To build these collaboration skills, a data science professional should seek opportunities to practice public speaking and could seek feedback from professional mentors from different backgrounds and industries.

Most data products will be used by and affect a diverse set of external or internal end users, so they should be built by a diverse team. Data science professionals must be able to collaborate with technical and nontechnical teammates alike to ensure the final product is ethically and appropriately designed for the context of use. Even within the data science profession, there is a wide variety of disciplines: computer scientists, statisticians, mathematicians, engineers, economists, psychologists, linguists, and more may be at the table. A collaborative team benefits from the knowledge and literature from each of these backgrounds, and team members can learn from each other's diverse experiences.

When I was just starting out, I benefited greatly from working closely with teammates senior to me who generously shared their knowledge and helped me learn more quickly. I will always highly value team members who are willing to learn from others and share their own knowledge. A collaborative team composed of a variety of disciplines could together fulfill the previously mentioned laundry list of data science qualifications.

Seeking Continuous Improvement

Data science and the volume of data have come a long way since the first few articles about the impending data talent shortages were published by *Harvard Business Review* and others in 2012. There are multiple ways to skin the cat, but with evolving technology, there is often a better way. Data science teams that strive for continuous improvement can provide the most value and compete in quickly moving markets. An individual professional should be seeking out articles, books, online learning, and more not only to fill their own knowledge gaps, but also to learn about new tools and techniques that could be useful to their team.

A prospective data analyst, data engineer, or data scientist may be daunted by the list of concepts they have to learn, but it is most important to focus on building discipline, collaboration skills, and a plan for continuous improvement. This is good news! Developing these skills depends on grit and positive attitude, not extensive knowledge. Teams are strengthened by a diversity of perspective and backgrounds. Members who can collaborate and communicate effectively bring a lot of value to the table.

There will always be an abundance of problems for creative, smart people to solve with new algorithms. Let's just all be sure to check our code over one last time before we commit it!

Jen Heider is part of the data and analytics team at Huntington Bank. After graduating as the pilot student for the Ohio State University BS industrial and systems engineering data and analytics track, she began her career as a data science consultant at IBM, where she built her data science skills on projects across multiple industries. She then went on to work as a data scientist at Express. Jen is currently pursuing her MS in the ISE data and analytics track at OSU part-time while working for Huntington. Jen also volunteers as co-coordinator for Women in Machine Learning & Data Science Columbus and as logistics coordinator for the Women in Analytics Conference. In her free time, Jen loves reading, running, and outdoor activities of all kinds.

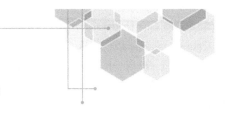

Ruth Milligan
Founder
Articulation

Building a Storytelling Culture Inside Data and Analytics

Introduction

Let's start with why storytelling matters in data and analytics. Brad Lemons, the SVP of customer insights and analytics at Nationwide Insurance, is known to say to his team, "If you can't sell your insights, they are worthless. Storytelling is not an option, it is a requirement." Likewise, Scott Berinato, senior editor of *Harvard Business Review*, argues that storytelling is one of six "musts" for a strong data science organization. But it persists nonetheless as an unresolved competence gap, with only a few shining examples.

Storytelling reveals data insights and analytics science. After completing the rigorous problem-solving and data analysis for a business challenge, it is our best chance of synthesizing the insight to advance key business objectives.

Storytelling is an art, not a science. Yet analytics professionals tend to be scientists, not artists. The innate ability to understand how people hear and listen is not usually a fluency among the scientific set of analytics practitioners. It demands use of emotion, appealing to the senses so that people can remember and repeat what was shared. It is no less rigorous than science, however, in that a strong story requires rounds of iteration and feedback to ensure it supports the key insights.

Three Roadblocks to Becoming a Storyteller

After spending several years coaching and training storytelling inside data and analytics teams, I've observed three barriers that hold back analytics teams from becoming great storytellers.

Problem #1: Lack of Structured Thinking That Supports the Story
Storytelling is a support for a larger message and insight. Storytelling is not the deliverable; it is a vehicle to make the deliverable accessible and memorable. Getting to the story is fueled only by strong organization of the data that answers a specific question on the audience's mind.

The preeminent process for organizing thinking was introduced in the 1970s by Barbara Minto in her book *The Pyramid Principle*. She argues that people use the writing process to formulate their thinking. Although the idea is likely somewhere in the mess of the words — or visualizations in the world of analytics — the insight is lost to the reader or listener. As an executive at McKinsey, Minto helped shape a culture of organized thinkers, which still is dominant today in every McKinsey presentation.

In short, structured thinking is the ability to concisely and impactfully organize what you want to say before you write or say it. This step — what I call content framing or "staging" — is a difficult and oft-ignored practice in data and analytics teams. The process of organizing data and charts showing a lot of careful science is more the practice, less the key takeaways of what the audience cares about against a larger business objective or issue.

But although Minto's structured thinking process was groundbreaking, it did not include the emotional, connecting vehicle of storytelling. What hierarchical thinking does allow for is the ability to "bottom line" a message. In the first two minutes of a presentation, it tells us that Cinderella got her glass slipper and Prince Charming (the insight, the concluding thought). Whereas the stories that led to that conclusion (evil stepsisters, attending the ball) reveal more as the audience desires or time allows.

It is not uncommon to hear this comment from scientists and researchers at the top of their field who are asked to use hierarchical thinking strategies in developing a talk or presentation: "I've never learned to deliver information like this. I've always been taught that I reveal the insight at the end, not the beginning." Indeed, the process forces a hard turn away from the typical science talk, where you slowly reveal your problem, hypotheses, scientific process, control groups, early results, and final insights, in that order. For lay audiences, the process is reversed.

Problem #2: Lack of Exposure to Structured Thinking or Storytelling
Students graduating from undergraduate and graduate programs with a focus in data science or analytics are not exposed to structured thinking or storytelling, let alone encouraged to practice it. In a review of the top 15 master's programs in data and analytics in the U.S., online curricula and course listings revealed that only three of them offered any class on communication. Of those two, one of them was a component of a larger project that focused on leadership.

Companies are hiring very smart data scientists who "skipped the class," as I am known to say. In other words, they are coming to teams without the most fundamental skill sets in structured thinking or storytelling.

The first step in any structured thought sequence is to deeply understand what the audience already knows, the questions they desire answered, and what outcome you want them to take. And most scientists are incredibly used to communicating with their own audiences but not ones that don't speak their language.

It isn't just exposure to the methodologies of structured thinking and storytelling that is important. Practicing in front of diverse audiences helps reinforce the idea that it isn't about you, it's about them.

An analytics team at a large financial institution was to report on their progress on goals to their leadership. Because it was an annual review, it required an unusually large amount of data to be curated and organized. There were 200 people who had contributing roles in this review. The organizer gave them each two slides to present. Those, added to the deck of other insights, totaled 438 pages. When I asked what slide they got through in the meeting, you may have guessed it: Slide 3.

Problem #3: Feedback, or Lack Thereof

Let's face it, people are really bad at giving constructive feedback. I was once on a call with a senior risk executive, who told me it was easier to redo his associates' presentations than teach them a new way. No surprise, the call was a cry to help him pull out of the black hole he had created.

Mike Manocchia, the analytics director at Cigna, encourages his team members to attend their peers' presentations — even if it isn't their internal client or project — so they can give their colleagues productive feedback. It is critical to provide this feedback promptly so presenters can correct their behavior in future presentations.

Giving and receiving feedback are also intrinsically tied to knowing your audience. When analysts get feedback that they didn't "meet the mark" on delivering an insight, it might be that the insight was true or accurate, but it did not address the question on their audience's mind. Therefore, it was deemed irrelevant.

A senior analytics leader was giving part of a presentation inside a sales pitch. Her job was to show the potential customer insight trends at other companies and how this company could embrace the same analysis in order to grow their business. But in the middle of the presentation, she was tapped to sit down by her boss. The chairman in the room had become increasingly frustrated with the content, which was not answering the prospects' questions. Because the analytics leader was focused on finishing the presentation, she missed their cues.

The analytics team didn't win the pitch (because of pricing), but this moment was devastating for the young executive. In an evaluation of "what happened," it was revealed that the team had only set aside time to practice the night before. And although they knew what their main contacts were interested in, no one took time to appreciate the points of view of the chairman who controlled the meeting.

Four Core Storytelling Principles

Aside from the obvious answer — "more training" — what can leaders do to bring good storytelling behaviors inside their teams? Let's look at four driving principles I believe accelerate teams to be more efficient and engaging in their storytelling and general presentation skills.

Content

Definition: The data being used to develop the presentation.

When this is a challenge: When the audience's intentions are not clear as to the questions they want answered, making organizing the key message focus difficult.

Time

Definition: The time allowed to prepare for a presentation.

When this is a challenge: When the amount of content and need to synthesize/iterate is larger than the time allowed to do it.

Development

Definition: The opportunity to iterate with appropriate feedback with the audience in mind.

When this is a challenge: When those giving feedback don't have a development mindset and can only make suggestions based on their own anxieties, not on the growth of the storyteller/speaker.

Space

Definition: The willingness to fail.

When this is a challenge: In cultures that expect things to be "done" on a first iteration — and for people driven to perform perfectly all the time. Although you may block out time and accept feedback, "space" gives you room to try new things, accept failure, and try again.

Conclusion

Storytelling is necessary for your analytics insights to be heard, understood, and adopted. For that to happen, however, leaders need to create a culture in which to teach, foster, and reinforce good storytelling across the entire team. That means affording time, development, and space for teams to improve.

The investment is worth it. These skills are difficult to learn, but they are wildly efficient and effective when mastered. I like to say you always live in choice: Pay now or pay later. If you don't "pay now" for the time and effort required to build these storytelling characteristics, you will "pay later" when your analytics insights aren't adopted and you have to constantly redo work.

Ruth Milligan is an executive communication coach who specializes in coaching and training executives in structured thinking, storytelling, public speaking, and oral defense strategies. She has coached over 1,000 speakers on speaking engagements ranging from keynote speeches to short pitches and hundreds of TEDx talks. (She is one of the longest-running TEDx organizers.) Ruth is passionate about helping people find their voice and tell their story, especially in areas related to data and analytics. She has been an original partner to Women in Analytics, helping to elevate all of the conference speakers through the WIA Speaker Academy.

Ruth is a graduate of Miami University (BA, speech communication) and runs a professional practice, Articulation, which serves Fortune 500 clients, nonprofits, and individuals across the United States.

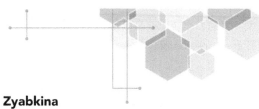

Tanya Zyabkina
Independent Consultant

How to Prioritize Analytical Projects

We all are swamped with requests, so how do we determine which ones are more important than others? Should we address the most urgent questions first or the ones with the most value for the business?

Having a good system to prioritize analytical projects is the key to producing relevant and meaningful analytical results. Analytics should not happen in a silo, and prioritization is a way to connect business objectives with the realities of analytical work. As Tom O'Toole wrote in *Harvard Business Review*, "business leaders and data scientists should jointly decide which business problems to focus on."[1]

Here are some factors that we need to take into account when prioritizing analytical projects.

Value of the Answer or the Analytical Solution

How much money is at stake? Behind every request, there is a business question, and we need to know the impact the answer can have on the bottom line.

When I managed the analytical side of direct mail for a major U.S. cable company, I got to analyze a wide variety of acquisition and upsell campaigns. Some were general market offers that had over a million targets. Others were international channel offers with fewer than 20,000 potential targets.

Even if the company were to perfect these niche mailings, it would have made barely enough money to pay for the versioning and analytics themselves.

The value of the solution was much greater for the large mail campaigns.

One exception to this rule is testing. Companies often test new approaches on a small segment, such as the 20,000 targets I mentioned, and when they find an optimal solution, they scale the program up. Therefore, when looking at the size of the question, don't forget how the solution can be leveraged at full scale.

Feasibility

How likely are you to reach a conclusion? Do you have or can you obtain the necessary data to make it work? Have you seen indications in your previous research that a solution is possible?

Some problems look easy on the surface. I remember watching one VP after another starting a project to connect an incoming sales call phone number and a new account. Every one of them failed because nobody knew how to make incompatible systems talk to each other.

I have seen analysts who had created excellent propensity-to-buy models stumble when creating a workable sales uplift model, despite using clean, reliable, and familiar data. The sales uplift from campaigns was not something they understood well, in part due to the small marginal impact of the campaigns on sales.

Failures that come when the data does not flow from one system into another are pretty common. This is particularly true for legacy systems and systems that use different data layouts.

Modeling can go off track when our target variable is complicated and we have not researched it well enough.

Some questions to answer when you assess the feasibility of projects:

- Do you have or can you obtain clean, reliable data?
- Are the data's granularity and latency acceptable?
- Do you know enough about the target variable or the process you are trying to model to come up with a reasonable hypothesis about its behavior?

Urgency

I have yet to meet a non-urgent analytics request. Jokes aside, many requests are in fact urgent, and that should factor into request prioritization.

It is important to communicate to the business that there is a relationship between the turnaround time and the quality of the result. In many cases, the business will reveal its priorities on whether waiting longer for a better answer is worth it.

Watch out for boomerang questions! Under the pressure of a pending decision, the business often chooses a quick-and-dirty answer to a fundamental question. However, if the question helps inform a recurring or regular business decision (e.g., which offer do we send to this segment?), it will come back to haunt you until it is fully answered.

When I was first asked to figure out how much a cable bill should go up after a promotion expires, my recommendation was to get a partial answer from a quick analysis but also to run a proper pricing test that would have lasted 18 months. Understandably, a test that lasted 18 months did not fit the business time frame, and the second half of my recommendation was ignored. Three years later, the company was still grappling with the same half-answered question. As it turns out, the company ended up spending more time to obtain a less certain answer.

Expected Quality of the Answer

When I was an analyst for a retail company, I was tasked with measuring the impact of a marketing program for new store openings. The assignment was a collection of worst-case scenarios: the number of observations (new stores) was low, the new stores had no last-year basis on which to judge their sales, and their initial sales differed widely from the forecast made before the openings. On top of that, the sales in the first weeks tended to rise steeply but unevenly, thus obfuscating the impact of the program.

I spent a lot of time trying to figure out how to clean the sales data from the effects of all those confounding variables, but the results were still hardly certain. To make matters worse, the business outright rejected adjusting the sales for seasonality, mainly because the seasonality was helping the results look better at the time. The measurement was not just imprecise, it was biased.

Fortunately, I only had to wait four months before temperatures dropped and the seasonality adjustment was back on the table. By then, I managed to convince the business that the value of the question was not high enough to argue over. If a new store marketing program was the right thing to do, it should continue despite uncertainty in the numbers.

Here are a few things to think of when assessing the quality of the answer:

- Is your sample size large enough to ensure the right precision of measurement?
- Does your analysis have built-in biases, or is it otherwise misleading?
- Will the answer be trivial?
- Are there other ways to answer the question or address the need?

Effort

Business people are often unaware of how much effort it takes to produce different types of analysis, and their requests are usually resource-agnostic. Clearly communicating the effort level, turnaround time, and alternative ways to answer the question is an important part of analytical work. This is the same approach used when assessing the urgency of the request, and the business needs to participate in the discussion of effort versus turnaround options.

At some point in their career, every analyst is asked to answer the most trivial question using the most unreliable, inaccessible, and latent data. Hone your communication skills so you can educate your business counterparts about the level of effort and offer reasonable alternatives that will make the project go faster and easier for all.

Ease of Integration into the Business

Your solution is worth nothing if it can't be effectively integrated into how the company does its business. I have seen an analytical solution flop simply because it was served to busy customer service representatives in a system that they considered distracting. Most either had it turned off or learned to ignore the prompts.

When thinking about the end result of your work, you have to research how to present it best. If your output is a presentation, make sure to create clear recommendations for the business with visualizations to back them up. If you are sending your results into another system, learn how it works and how your data will be consumed.

Whether It Informs or Enables Other Analytical Projects

Analytical insights don't live in isolation. They feed into each other and build upon each other, and one answer makes many others possible. While most questions asked by the business are "applied," some information that feeds the answers is "fundamental."

In my prior work, I came upon one such fundamental question about the relationship between subscriber behavior and tenure. Subscriber tenure was a big factor in every disconnect analysis, from pricing to service updates. Yet up to that point, nobody had looked at this relationship in depth because the analysis could not answer a specific question, other than feeding someone's curiosity.

A subsequent deep dive on tenure opened up a wealth of insight that helped improve disconnect reporting, facilitated rate increase and promotion expiration analyses, and fed into disconnect propensity models, along with other analytical projects. The insights from this analysis paid for themselves many times over in saved time and better analytical results.

What Do You Do If You Are Swamped With Data Requests?

Many analysts find themselves getting so many data requests that prioritization seems daunting. Here are some recommendations for speeding up analytical delivery:

- Standardize common answers. There are good ways to answer the most frequently asked questions, and these ways need to be agreed upon, standardized, and documented.
- Automate standardized reports. Look for ways to produce standard assessments faster by automating them. Staging input data so that it can be easily processed and packaged as answers to common questions will shorten turnaround time for many requests.
- When faced with an urgent, non-standard, heavy-effort request, offer to substitute a standardized answer that provides most of the requested information. Since standardized data is more reliable, and the turnaround time is much shorter, these substitutions make a lot of sense for both the business and the analytics department.

Conclusion

Project prioritization is an integral part of analytical work. When you don't explicitly engage in prioritization, the projects still get prioritized, often based on urgency.

Explicit prioritization work opens the dialogue with your business counterparts about their objectives, and it leads to better alignment of analytics with your organization's goals. The process forces you to look at a bigger picture of analytics delivery. As a result, you will better understand the gaps in analytical capabilities and form ideas on how you can deliver the analytics your company will need in the future.

Tanya Zyabkina helps companies make better decisions based on data. Her 15 years of corporate experience were focused on producing insights that impacted business strategy at multiple Fortune 500 companies in the retail and telecom industries. Her work spans from qualitative market research in the fashion industry to determining the impact of promotions for a cable provider. Tanya's passion is figuring out which programs deliver value for a company, be that a visit by a technical specialist or a new merchandise assortment. Her work for Victoria's Secret covered brand image analytics and CRM program effectiveness. At AutoZone, she determined the impact that changing automotive technologies had on the long-term KPIs of the company. As a director of marketing analytics at Time Warner Cable, she led a team that tackled complex analytical problems in marketing, pricing, customer service, and retention. Tanya holds an MBA from The Ohio State University, a master's degree in economics from Novosibirsk State University, and a graduate certificate in data science from Harvard Extension School. She publishes her thoughts on analytics on her web-site zyabkina.com.

Reference

[1]O'Toole, Tom. "What's the Best Approach to Data Analytics?" *Harvard Business Review*, 2 March 2020. (https://hbr.org/webinar/2020/03/the-best-approach-to-data-analytics)

Lori Silverman
Founder/CEO and Shift Strategist, Adjunct Professor
Partners for Progress®; Golden Gate University

The Unspoken Reason Behind Analytics Efforts Not Gaining Full Traction

If I asked in a public forum how successful your enterprise's analytics efforts are, how would you reply? If I asked again off the record, behind closed doors, what would you confide to me?

Are you aware, to this day, that not one study from any source demonstrates analytics efforts are *consistently producing* actionable results? The one study showcasing the best results is Accenture's August 2019 *Closing the Data Gap* study.[1] After two decades of focus on big data, 32% of 190 U.S. executives state they're able to create measurable value from data, while 27% said their data and analytics projects produce actionable results.

Really? That's it after 20 years? How disappointing.

Reinforcing this characterization, the foreword to NewVantage Partners' 2020 survey of C-suite executives on connecting data/AI investments to business outcomes says, "The survey results have been quite consistent [over the years] ... the field is struggling to succeed despite massive investments in technology and applications."[2] How can this be? Think of all the billions of dollars that enterprises have sunk into these efforts:

- Hiring, orienting, and training full-time analytics/data science staff, along with their leaders, and standing up varied analytics, business intelligence, data science, and data functions.

- Bringing in diverse technologies and applications, some of which you may be helping to implement: data collection, data warehousing, data cleansing, business intelligence, data visualization and analytics, and data marketplaces to house all data once it's all been cleaned. (Side note: Covid-19 taught us that historical data, at best, is suspect. A lot isn't usable/applicable anymore; ask those in the airline industry who do seat pricing.)
- A diverse IT group that's focused on securing technology and applications in the name of digitization, security/privacy, or "improving efficiencies" — which may unwittingly silo parts of key business processes, making data access frustrating.

What's the first inclination when these investments don't pay off? We say, "People are the problem." They don't use the right tools, aren't fully trained, don't attach their analytics work to overall strategy, or don't speak the language of the business. We blame leaders, saying they aren't supportive — because they don't know how to read, analyze, and interpret data. Are leaders truly not supportive? Or are they merely reacting to not getting what they need to make decisions fast enough?

The NewVantage Partners study offers a different slant, saying one outcome hasn't changed in the last eight years: "Organizations are not becoming data-driven and are not building data-focused cultures." The impediments in Accenture's study are also cultural and operational. Supporting this view is *Corinium's 2020 State of Data and Analytics US* report,[3] which concludes, "The challenge for data and analytics leaders will be to change the culture within their organizations to embed data-driven insights permanently into key business processes."

Do these studies mean we should immediately start work on shifting enterprise culture? Yes. And no.

Henry Ford once said, "If you always do what you've always done, you'll always get what you've always got." Perhaps it's also true here.

Why a "Data-Centric" Culture Isn't the Answer

What if we haven't been embracing the right mental model? Hear me out.

What if being data-centric isn't the right paradigm through which we should be viewing analytics work? What if being data-focused isn't the right culture to put in place enterprise-wide? What if being data-driven is akin to saying the solar system revolves around the earth, when what we really should be focused is on being "decision-first," which is akin to the solar system revolving around the sun?

Think about it: data serves decision-making; decision-making doesn't serve data. The same is true of technology. Technology serves decision-making; decision-making doesn't serve technology. Data (or technology) in these contexts is an "input," not the outcome/result. Why are we so overwhelmingly focused on the input?

Maybe we have put the cart before the horse. As a result, a data-centric mindset is the root cause of an inability to consistently produce actionable results from analytics work.

On the surface, this mindset shift to decision-first might seem trivial. As one who's helped transform entire enterprises in this manner, starting in the late 1980s, I know from experience it's not. To clarify, becoming a decision-first enterprise is more expansive than decision modeling, decision automation, decision science, decision intelligence, and decision management. It's about reframing the totality of what happens in an enterprise through a decision-making lens.

Here's one example. Why is there a push for data democratization — giving staff access to data they need to do their jobs? Does giving everyone access to data (via self-service analytics) imply they'll use it? We all know this isn't the case. Why aren't we promoting decision democratization instead, where those closest to a business decision and its implementation get the authority to make it, using the data linked to informing these decisions? Might this heighten their desire to produce actionable results while also culturally serving to empower them?

Now imagine if we substituted the word "decision" for "data" in these contexts:

- Decision governance versus data governance
- Decision visualization (mapping the elements of a decision) versus data visualization
- "Can the decision be trusted?" versus "Can the data be trusted?"

How would these mindset shifts change the nature of the conversations that you're having today?

Let's chat about what decision-first means in a global sense. Decision-first enterprises are driven to continually enhance consumers' experiences; they aren't driven by Fourth Industrial Revolution messaging (tech hype). Depending on your enterprise's focus, consumers may be end users, customers, employees, suppliers/vendors, investors, regulators, and/or the community at large. Think about this on a micro scale: how often do you remind people to tie their work back to the end user's use of the data for decision-making purposes? Wouldn't it be more fruitful to start with, "What's the decision(s) you're trying to make/inform?" — especially before creating another dashboard?

Our objective in helping the enterprise to become decision-first is to embed an enterprise core competence for collaborative data-informed decision-making throughout every nook and cranny of the organization. This is where culture comes into play. Keep in mind that the data literacy efforts being proposed today are about enhancing an individual's core competence with data. No matter how many people are trained on data collection, analysis, visualization, or more sophisticated tools/techniques, this will never be sufficient to create the enterprise core competence for smarter, accelerated decision-making. (On a side note, I know of no educational institution that offers a data/business analytics, data science, or business intelligence degree/certificate from a decision-centric perspective; they're all data-centric in design.)

Why should you take on spearheading this paradigm shift in your organization? Because it will help create a more intelligent and adaptive enterprise that better serves all stakeholder groups (outlined above), which will in turn aid the organization in achieving its strategies and operational goals. This helps address three key questions:

1. What's the cost of making a wrong decision?
2. Can we afford to take as much time as needed to make the right decision?
3. What's the cost of not fully implementing a decision once it's been made?

Creating a Decision-First Culture

Let's revisit culture. How do you create the groundswell for embedding this enterprise core competence into the DNA of the organization? On an individual level, you can:

- Ask questions. In meetings, ask: "What's the one decision we have to walk out of here having made?" When asked for data, respond: "How do we plan to use it?"
- Get training on collaborative data-informed decision-making and use the methodology with others.
- Map decision elements and processes before acquiring data. Decision intelligence can help here.

Simultaneously, what can you do to begin shifting the enterprise? Start by taking the following steps:

1. Strategically identify kindred spirits. Enlist them in doing what I suggested above.
2. Discuss with them the implications of a decision-first mindset for the organization. Then, co-create the first draft of a "vision story" that makes this transformation feel real, tangible, and desirable.
3. Socialize enterprise leaders to the vision story. Get their feedback and revise it.

4. Using this revised story as a guidepost, lead an "organizational architecture" assessment of each aspect of the enterprise — strategy, workflow/processes, policies, asset infrastructure, technology/data, external relationships, values/beliefs, people infrastructure, leadership practices, stakeholders — you get the gist. If you work for a larger enterprise, such as a multinational, conduct the assessment by business unit. Position it as a first-pass assessment to get a feel for what to strengthen or change; more depth and detail can be added over time. Seek out someone with expertise in organizational development for assistance.

5. From this, develop the first steps of a draft transformation plan and begin to work it. View the assessment and plan as iterative and organic; you'll be gaining input and feedback, and more involvement, from others over time.

6. Start teaching staff and leaders an approach for collaborative data-informed decision-making, while also gaining their input and feedback on steps 3 and 4.

Throughout all the steps, make sure the words and practices you use are framed from a decision-first perspective.

Reorienting the Analytics Universe

If we don't shift our paradigm from data-centric to decision-first, next year's research on the success of analytics efforts won't differ from previous studies. I realize it took almost 100 years for mainstream thinking to embrace Copernicus's view that the planets revolve around the sun. Only, I don't have 100 years to wait for success. Do you? What about your enterprise? Let's get started!

As the shift strategist and CEO of Partners for Progress, Lori Silverman has helped enterprises from 16 to 1 million employees navigate messy, complex changes and strategize about their future. Clients across 25 industries include Chevron, McDonalds, Target, American Family Insurance, Wells Fargo, Phillips North America, and the U.S. Air Force. Lori has inspired thousands to take action through her 90+ keynotes and hundreds of workshops. She has authored five books, most recently Business Storytelling for Dummies, and is known worldwide for her work in collaborative data-informed decision-making — a part of what she calls Data Literacy 2.0. Lori is an adjunct professor in Golden Gate University's Industrial and Organizational Psychology Master's Program, teaching the only I/O psychology course in the world on strategic thinking.

References

[1]Vasal, Ajay, et al. *Closing the Data-Value Gap. Accenture*, 2019.
(www.accenture.com/_acnmedia/pdf-108/accenture-closing-data-value-gap-fixed.pdf).

[2]Davenport, Thomas. H, and Randy Bean. Foreword to *Big Data and AI Executive Survey 2020*.
NewVantage Partners, 2020.
(https://c6abb8db-514c-4f5b-b5a1-fc710f1e464e.filesusr.com/ugd/e5361a_579e07bcb351420f-b9c24f28237fc6f5.pdf).

[3]2020 *State of Data & Analytics US*. Corinium, 2020.
(www.coriniumintelligence.com/reports/2020-soda-us).

Madhu Srinivasan
Principal Consultant – Data Analytics & AI
WIPRO

Analytics Organization: Centralize or Decentralize?

Whenever you ask the head of an analytics function in any organization what their priorities are, you will often hear terms such as "self-service," "left shift," "user empowerment," "democratization of analytics," and so on. Regardless of how you interpret these terms, the underlying theme is the same. There is a conscious attempt to move the balance more toward the individual business units and away from the traditional centralized analytics IT team model.

The balance between the centralized IT model and decentralized empowerment has swung like a pendulum over the past decades. Traditionally, IT organizations have attempted to centralize the analytics book of work in a shared services model in order to reap the following benefits:

- Governance. Centralization makes it possible to maintain control over the onboarding and usage of data and IT resources.
- Cost optimization. As redundancies are eliminated, there is a potential for cost optimization.
- Resource utilization. In a centralized model, resources are better utilized, as there is scope for optimization across work streams. In a decentralized model, there are always some resources lying idle while others are overutilized.

In recent times, however, the balance is shifting more and more toward a decentralized model due to certain key trends.

Business decisions are being made directly based on the output of the analytical workload. When market scenarios change, which they do all the time, the turnaround time for implementing those changes — be they data science algorithms or BI reports — is too high for decision makers. Very often, by the time a change is implemented, the use case has already become outdated. It is critical for businesses to quickly implement new insights to maintain a competitive edge. So business users are willing to forgo certain efficiencies in favor of agility.

Business units within large organizations are evolving their own business models and character. This makes them feel they have unique requirements that are not applicable to other business units within the organization. As a result, they tend to build their own ecosystem and platforms.

While we can all agree that there is no ideal model, here are some factors to consider when deciding on the level of decentralization or democratization in your analytics organization.

Organization Model

The level of decentralization in the analytics organization often shadows the overall organization model. There are organizations in which the business units function almost like separate legal entities. This sovereignty may be instilled based on the line of business (e.g., credit cards, auto loans, mortgages for a retail bank) or by geography. Funding and budgeting are driven at the business unit level rather than by themes like analytics.

The convergence of the data and analytics functions is another deliberation that organizations grapple with. Some large companies have a separate CDO and CAO, both of whom report to the CEO. In some organizations, data engineering and architecture roll up to the CDO, while the analytics stream is buried as a subcomponent in the "digital" organization. In such cases, even if there is a shared services organization, there is a split between how data is managed and how insights are derived.

Business Sponsorship

It is quite common for businesses to invest a lot in analytic infrastructure — big data clusters, data science models, multiple BI platforms — but derive hardly any business benefits. One common cause for this disjunction is a lack of concerted direction and sponsorship from the top.

There is no single solution that addresses every challenge in an analytics organization. Every approach has certain drawbacks, and the tendency is for different business units to go with a different approach, which leads to silos. To achieve optimization, it is critical that individual business units be incentivized to make minor compromises and converge on a larger strategy. High-level sponsorship is critical to enabling this transformation.

The Analytics Organization's Primary Objective

The goals of an analytics organization may be many. But the primary focus often dictates the level of empowerment at the business unit level.

There are certain financial services and nonprofit organizations whose primary goal with regard to analytics is compliance from a regulatory perspective. Here, the analytics organization is synonymous with reporting, and the emphasis is more on data quality and governance than on agility. Such organizations would rather be accurate than fast. Here a more centralized model works.

On the other hand, there are next-gen digital organizations whose focus is on customer analytics and product development. For them, it is OK to get a few numbers wrong, but it is critical to roll out the insights faster. In such cases, the business tends to gravitate toward a highly decentralized model.

Pipeline Components

The pipeline for the analytics workload has multiple subcomponents: data architecture, semantic model, ETL pipelines, data quality and data preparation, storage, data enrichment, and visualization. The level of centralization can vary at each component level.

In my opinion, data architecture and semantic modeling should be as centralized as possible, with the scope at the highest level. However, the actual pipeline and analytics use cases should be closer to the definition of the smallest business unit. That's where business users have the freedom to define and implement use cases subject to the broader guidelines defined by the central organization.

Requirements Diversity

There are situations where the datasets and insights required by various business units are somewhat homogenous with definable variations. This allows standardization at the data source level and the evolution of a framework for analytics self-service. But this becomes an ordeal when each business unit has unique requirements demanding specialized datasets that have very little relevance to other business units.

Degree of Change to the Data Models

An extension of the previous point has to do with the stability of the data models involved in the analytics pipeline. In a traditional analytics organization, most insights were derived from transaction systems like ERP systems, in which the data models were relatively stable and changes were infrequent. In the modern environment, however, data is often federated from various sources, and data models are constantly changing. As a result, centralizing the data model is extremely complex.

Entitlement Requirements

There may be regulatory and business restrictions on the consumption of data and information from one business unit or region by another. While it is possible to implement fine-grained permission control and entitlement rules in the database and analytics platforms, when it comes to highly sensitive information, many organizations feel it is safer to build independent analytics environments for each business unit.

Data Literacy Levels

The promise of analytics democratization often assumes a high ratio of tech-savvy, data-literate business users. Despite the proliferation of technology and the increase of Millennials in the workplace, maturity in data literacy is still a distant dream. Most business users don't have either the necessary skills or the patience to reap the benefits of true self-service analytics. They often end up hiring other power users or sometimes data engineers/scientists in their team. This approach completely defeats the vision of decentralization.

When organizations attempt to increase the level of democratization or decentralization of their analytics function, they must ensure their training machinery is geared for continuous upskilling of their business users.

Madhu Srinivasan is a seasoned analytics professional with over 15 years of experience. She has advised several Fortune 500 companies on implementing data and analytics strategies. She co-founded a startup that specialized in data and collaboration. She is a regular contributor to various knowledge forums.

Ursula Cottone
Chief Data & Architecture Officer
Huntington Bank

Collaboration: A Key Ingredient to Success

Being a chief data officer poses several challenges, from the definition and boundaries of the role to ever-changing technologies and business priorities. However, I've found the antidote is collaboration. For a CDO to truly be effective enterprise-wide, support from the most senior level is critical from the beginning. Listening is key to comprehending the challenges the enterprise is facing, how stakeholders view data, what they want to do in the future. This listening will allow you to translate pain points and aspirational goals into an overarching data strategy and explain how you can help the enterprise.

In my current position, I spent my first couple of months meeting with senior leaders, my peers, and colleagues throughout the company to listen. I met with over 150 people in an effort to understand their priorities, needs, and pain points, as well as learn about the culture, including the language of the bank. It was imperative to accurately grasp the current needs, issues, and goals from all perspectives so I could construct a data strategy that translates into solutions that are meaningful and address challenges for colleagues at all levels. This understanding and the relationships I began building are key to true collaboration. Those you interact with need to know you understand and are interested in them and their work.

Senior leadership of a bank can include upward of a dozen individuals, so it is critically important to build a small team of sponsors/advocates for the data strategy. It will look different for each CDO because of organizational structure and those individuals who are most interested in data. For me, my mini board of directors includes the head of technology and operations, our chief financial officer, and our chief risk officer. These leaders ensure I stay on point with the bank's overall strategy and understand the funding landscape, and they act as a sounding board for my strategy and roadmap.

Establishing Governance

Once the building of relationships was underway, it was important to define clear data-related roles and responsibilities throughout IT, operations, and the business. These definitions allow colleagues to engage at the right level and understand how we are going to work together. This is most effectively done through a data governance and management structure. I first rely on senior leadership to support the data strategy by allocating resources, providing funding, and deciding on key issues. I also rely on their support as I create a committee structure that includes senior leaders from every area of the organization.

Once you've engaged your senior leadership team and gained their support, it's important to structure a governing committee composed of key business leaders/executives and risk, audit, information security, and other stakeholders. I rely on this committee to offer advice, drive prioritization of our efforts, allocate resources, and provide ongoing feedback. Committee members also serve in a governance capacity, approving the data management policy and reviewing and reacting to policy violations.

Once you've established a governance structure, it's important to grow this network, drawing in those who are connected more closely to the data, applications, and source systems. These stakeholders (i.e., trustees/stewards/curators) collaborate to identify, prioritize, escalate, and implement fixes for data-related issues. Collaboration is key not just with the stakeholders, but among and between them. Our work in the Chief Data Office is to engage these stakeholder colleagues by listening to their challenges, bringing them together to learn from one another, and maintaining engagement. We engage these stakeholders through recurring meetings to discuss data-related challenges they have and to share our progress against these issues tied back to our data strategy.

Sustaining Momentum

With the work underway, sustaining momentum requires a significant amount of two-way communication. Our story as a Chief Data Office should always be evolving, so we must continually engage stakeholders at all levels by sharing our vision and progress. We do this through several channels.

First, our roadmap and strategy are continually refreshed and updated — on a quarterly basis, at a minimum. I then share our progress — what's been completed, what's new, and what's next — through "roadshow" meetings with a broad invitee list of our designated data stakeholders and other interested colleagues at least twice a year. I also frequently share our story and strategy in town halls, all-hands meetings, forums, and team meetings throughout business and IT. And if it isn't obvious, I keep the company's senior leadership updated by sharing our progress. It's important to continually share at all levels.

Collaboration also needs to occur within the team directing and executing the work. These colleagues and the way they collaborate are what allow us to deliver against our goals. It's important that we have the right processes, standards, and measurement tools in place to understand how we manage data, what our current-state maturity is, and what our future-state goal is. We address this in a number of ways:

- Data quality and maturity assessments. We've used EDM's Data Management Capability Assessment Model (DCAM) to benchmark the current-state maturity of our data management and governance capabilities and target our future-state goal.
- Policy and standards. With the support and approval of our governance committee structure, we've developed a relevant and actionable data policy and supporting standards, which are revisited annually.
- Data management and quality tooling. A robust data quality framework enables trusted data and addresses root causes of data quality issues. It also provides business insights used to improve customer experience and reduce risk. This includes the processes and tooling necessary to

support critical data elements, metadata, the business glossary, master data, and data quality.

Our work in the Chief Data Office couldn't be done without the day-to-day partnership of our technology and architecture teams. We drive the enterprise data strategy and roadmap and are responsible for data quality, governance, reporting, data capabilities, and business intelligence. Our partners in tech and architecture are responsible for information governance, infrastructure, data acquisition, and sourcing. Together, we all work together to deliver on business and IT demand against our data strategy.

Making Collaboration Routine

This dynamic between multiple groups who succeed or who fail together can be challenging, especially for a newer team. Building routines that drive collaboration is one way we've managed the challenge. Our collective leadership team meets multiple times per week in a variety of forums designed to discuss specific topics, business case reviews, risk management updates, project reviews, colleague calibration, and new work/intake. We also hold Data Summits, which allow us to look forward and to assess what's going well, what could be improved, and what's next on our roadmap. In addition, we have cross-team 1:1s to build deeper relationships among the colleagues who work closest together. Lastly, we conduct combined town halls and fun activities (potlucks, fundraisers, spirit days, etc.) to help build the connections that drive the kind of collaboration needed to succeed.

Collaboration is key to managing change and ensuring the ongoing support of our stakeholders for the ultimate success of our data strategy. We continue to focus on the talent throughout the organization, the strategy of the bank, and the needs of our stakeholders. Collaboration requires a strong dedication to listening to people and sharing the information that is relevant to them.

As the chief data and architecture officer at Huntington Bank, Ursula Cottone is focused on driving business-focused outcomes, including improving the customer experience, growing revenues, driving operational efficiency, and reducing risk for the bank. In addition, she is dedicated to solving reporting and analytic pain points by executing against an enterprise data strategy and delivering the necessary capabilities. Her goal is to have Huntington actively manage data as an enterprise asset in order to make lives better, help businesses thrive, and strengthen the communities the bank serves.

Ursula brings to Huntington more than 25 years of experience in banking, in a variety of roles across business segments and technology, including eight years as a CDO. Prior to joining Huntington, Ursula was the CDO at Citizens Bank. She also spent 17 years at Key Bank, where she held various roles of increasing responsibility, including chief administrative officer for capital markets, shared services leader, and CDO.

Ursula holds a BS from Bowling Green State University and an MBA from Cleveland State University. In addition, she is a graduate of the Stonier Graduate School of Banking and the University of Chicago Strategic Business Leadership Program.

Ursula is currently on the board of directors for Directions for Youth and Families in Columbus, Ohio. She moved to the Columbus area in 2018 and resides in Grandview Heights, Ohio, with her dog, Oliver.

Selma Dogic
Lead Self-Service Analytics
Carter's

From the Business Case to the People Case: How the Right People in the Right Places Can Transform Your Organization

Our data landscape is transforming, so why isn't our data strategy? Over the decades, the world has seen shifts in the way that consumers live, work, and play, yet consumer behavior is not the only thing that has driven industries to transform. Customers are consuming and producing much more data than ever before. Every click translates into hundreds of data points, yet our ability to capitalize on those data points and make meaningful deductions from them lags far behind in the transformation. Transforming the old operational model to be data-driven isn't a matter of profit and loss any longer — it is a matter of sustainability.

Albeit daunting in itself, transforming operations and organizations to be better driven by data is even more difficult without a sound strategy. A strategy that keeps an organization's most important asset — its people — at the core is the one most likely to succeed. Data is just data without the right teams making sense of it.

Making the People Case

Here I make the case that the right analytics strategy consists of three things, all of which are focused on the people case. First, I propose positioning business units to conduct their own descriptive analytics. Second, I recommend curating analytics use cases/projects to only those that have a business champion and a quantified business impact. Third, I argue that each analytics project needs to have three roles dedicated to it: the data translator, data storyteller, and data scientist.

To position business units to conduct their own descriptive analytics, data and the tools that are used to analyze it need to be democratized and federated. Requiring partnerships between IT departments and business units, the organization must enable business analysts to access, analyze, and deliver insights. This frees more advanced practitioners to move beyond heuristics to advanced analytics. Essentially, by empowering business analysts, the data scientists have the capacity to conduct true data science and move an organization toward analytical maturity.

Champions are paramount to a successful strategy because they are vital to change management. Data science drives meaning when it can influence an organization to modify its behavior. This is only possible when the business implication is clear and a leader is championing that change. Champions are leaders in the organization that can shape the direction of the business and their peers. Champions also drive adoption. Without a clear business case and champion, the analytics project is doomed to fail because its return on investment will be unclear to business leaders and thus will not elicit change. Without this role, data science projects will merely sit on the shelf while the business maintains the status quo.

An essential element of the people case is clear delineation of roles and responsibilities. The *data translator* clearly articulates the purpose and outcomes of the analytics use case and models. This role differs from a champion in that the data translator belongs to the analytics team. Rather than being an organizational leader, the data translator is an analytics leader. This person also ensures that the recommendations and outcomes derived from the analytical use case can be feasibly implemented by the business. The *data storyteller* clearly delivers the analytical results for consumption. Whether this be through presentations, white papers, or dashboards, this individual delivers insights that are easy for the audience to understand and act on. Fully dedicated to data modeling, the *data scientist* is well versed in machine learning techniques and has a deep understanding of statistics. As a team, these individuals should be immersed in the business to better understand the problem at hand and the viability of their proposed solution. Agility and scale are achieved through this clear alignment on roles.

A People-Centered Strategy

Conducting fast and sound analytics is difficult. It's even more difficult without a strategy. Transforming an organization to a state of analytics maturity is no mean feat. Yet when we focus on enabling and empowering the right people, the work becomes much more feasible.

Companies are realizing that analytics is no longer a "nice to have"; rather it's fundamental. Organizations that are unable to move at the speed of business — those that are ill-equipped to respond to consumer changes — are losing their ability to compete. Those that are committed to embracing data as an asset will not only win for their customers, but they will also win for their people.

Selma Dogic leads self-service analytics at Carter's. She works with business teams to drive insights and tell data stories more effectively. She serves as the data translator and works to bridge the gaps between IT and business analytics. Selma has been a part of data science teams at both The Home Depot and NCR. Prior to that, she worked in state and local consulting. Selma received an MS in economics from the Georgia Institute of Technology (Georgia Tech). She served as one of GeorgiaForward's Young Gamechangers and, in 2018, received NCR's CFO Excellence award.

Kristin McClure
Chief Data Officer
State of Vermont

Building a Data-Oriented Decision-Making System

Effective decision-making is increasingly important to business performance and a differentiator between businesses that thrive and those that lag. The use of data and analytics has the power to improve the quality of decision-making, and the proliferation of data-oriented decision-making will continue across virtually every industry.

Good decisions are made using a blend of data, experience, and intuition — the mixture of which is dependent on the amount of high-quality data. Data-oriented decision-making strategy is contingent on three key characteristics: repeatable, sustainable, and automated.

Repeatable. A repeatable data collection and analysis process is one that can be reproduced time and time again with consistency and dependability. The process is not dependent on a single individual's skill to gather data. It should require little overhead or intervention to reproduce.

Sustainable. Conditions in most business environments change over time, and a healthy data collection and analytics system possesses the flexibility and scalability to adapt and perform across a range of different operating conditions as those environments change.

Automated. Systems that have dependencies on people to successfully perform a task are inherently at greater risk for failure due to error or changes in staff. Well-automated functions remove the variables of these risks that can compromise the availability and integrity of the data being collected and used for key organizational decisions.

Building a system that embodies the repeatable, sustainable, and automated characteristics can only be achieved if the data itself also conforms to a set of attributes:

- Data availability — How routinely and readily accessible is the data?
- Data operations — How reliable is the collection, processing, and storage of the data?
- Data quality — How relevant, timely, and error-free is the data?

Data availability. A good data-based decision-making system needs to be built with the customer in mind. Start from the end: what do customers and decision makers need to see to help inform good decision-making? In the case of Covid-19, this data has largely been: infection transmission modeling, data on the virus, and data on critical equipment (hospital status and PPE) and their associated supply chains.

With these needs understood, determine what data elements help best portray their condition. Initially, these data representations do not have to be highly refined; they do, however, have to be accurate. Less granular but valid data is far more valuable than a higher volume of data that is of lower quality — and therefore less trustworthy.

Data operations. Perhaps the most challenging aspect of operations is the enablement of data feeds that provide the basis for analysis and decision-making. While it's often time-consuming, if the data is not currently being collected, these connections must be built. A good goal for these data feeds is to seek the characteristics of repeatable, sustainable, and automated. Data feeds will need to be created at some frequency (depending on your goal) with a keen focus on the quality of the data being collected.

In my experience, data quality is the single largest determinant of success and adoption of a successful data-based decision-making process. High data quality will enable your organization to make the best decisions for short- and long-term success. Poor data quality can suboptimize decision-making and result in impacts that range from negligible to catastrophic.

While data quality is not as flashy to talk about as compared to approaches like predictive modeling, everything hinges on data quality. Consequently, it is vital to monitor data quality using key process indicators and to do this through various steps across the process, not just prior to publication. Having multiple points of data quality checks enables data quality issues to be found as close to the source as possible — and therefore to be more easily fixed.

Data quality. Once ongoing and sustainable data feeds are established and accompanied by KPIs to measure the health of the data, the data is now ready for use. Really spend time to understand the customers of the data. The users could be senior leadership, engineers, clients, or citizens. Work to understand the user base and give them what they need — even if they don't know what that is or how to ask for it.

Descriptive statistics are as important as effective visuals and should always be included. Show and share the data. It helps build both confidence and understanding for those using the data to base decisions upon.

Again, the data does not need to be highly refined from the start. An approach of continuous improvement to iterate upon the data being provided is very common, but in all cases, a consistent sharing of the core data will provide the most powerful benefits. This data sharing can come in the form of a report, a visual dashboard, or any number of other methods — but show the data!

I have found an approach where users can view and access the data whenever they need to is the most effective way to achieve this. Whatever means of data sharing is selected, it should be both easy to access and easy to use. Create visuals that are visually smart — meaning that they show the data, they tell the story, they do not mislead the audience, and they can be interpreted without explanation or narration. Let the data speak for itself and be prepared to tell the story of the data. That is the beauty of it: data tells a story, and good data delivery processes and tools enable our users to listen to the story.

Organizations of all sizes and missions are making the move toward data-based decision-making. The decision to embrace these practices in and of themselves does not improve the quality of the decisions being made. Only through a thoughtful design of a system that gathers the right kind of data, the right amount of data, with the right quality controls can that system provide the users with the insights needed to help inform good decision-making. As data leaders, it's essential that we help our customers and users navigate these complexities and allow them to focus on trusting and using the data to make the best decisions possible for their organizations and stakeholders.

Kristin McClure is currently the chief data officer for the State of Vermont and was recently named to the CDO Magazine 2020 List of Global Data Power Women. A data scientist with leadership expertise, Kristin has been involved in data-driven decision-making in the private sector for about 20 years. Her areas of focus include machine and deep learning algorithms (linear and logistic regression, decision trees, random forest, SVM, clustering, neural networks, feature engineering, and natural language processing) and data visualization. She has a master's degree in data science from Johns Hopkins, a certification in big data and social analytics from the Massachusetts Institute of Technology, and a bachelor's degree in economics from the University of Pennsylvania.

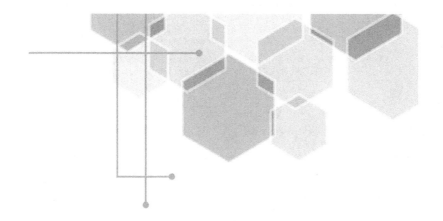

ETHICS

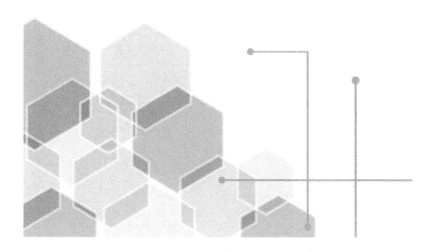

Rim Tehraoui
Group Chief Data Officer
BNP Paribas

Léa Deleris
Head of RISK Artificial Intelligence
Research

Bias in AI: A Mirror of Our Society?

Searching for patterns, filtering and processing them, making sense out of them, and taking decisions accordingly are what individuals do consciously or unconsciously each and every day of their lives. With artificial intelligence becoming more and more pervasive in our society, we expect it to do not only the same, but to do it even better.

A rapid overview of the media shows, however, that AI models of different shapes and forms have been seen to display bias in their output, treating people from different racial backgrounds or genders in different ways.

How Much Truth Is There to This Worrying Trend and What Are Its Root Causes?

In fall 2019, Apple's credit card, launched in August 2019 in partnership with Goldman Sachs, ran into major problems when users noticed that its machine learning algorithm seemed to offer smaller lines of credit to women than to men. The claims surfaced on social media after tech entrepreneur David Heinemeier Hansson tweeted that even though he and his spouse share assets and she has a higher credit score, Apple Card offered him 20 times the credit limit that it offered to her.

In the domain of image processing, image recognition algorithms have been reported to come to offensive conclusions when processing non-white complexions. For instance, an HP webcam, which included facial recognition software to automatically follow the position of the user, did not recognize a black person when he entered the picture. A similar technology embedded in a digital camera kept suggesting that Asian persons were blinking.

In a similar manner, a recent study from Stanford showed that five different speech-to-text technologies developed by Amazon, Google, IBM, Microsoft, and Apple had error rates that doubled between white speakers and African American ones.[1] Such technologies are currently being used for automatic screening in recruitment processes and as transcription tools for court hearings.

Finally, in natural language processing, machine translation models have been shown to incorporate gender stereotypes. Translating the sentence "He is a nurse; she is a doctor" from English to Hungarian and then back to English results in "She is a nurse; he is a doctor." More importantly, word-embedding models that capture semantic relationships in language — which have become fundamental building blocks for many NLP tasks — encode bias. One common example is the analogy derived from such models that "computer programmer is to homemaker as man is to woman."

There are many reasons why such biases appear in the output of the models chosen. Let's revisit our examples.

In the Apple Card case, Goldman Sachs argued that, first, the algorithm was vetted for potential bias by a third party and, second, that it does not use gender as an input. So how could it discriminate if no one ever tells it which customers are women and which are men? What the company failed to take into account is that it is entirely possible for ML algorithms to discriminate on gender, even when they are programmed to be "blind" to that variable. Actually, this is precisely what those algorithms excel at: finding latent features in data (i.e., features that are not used to train the models but that can be derived from the data used to train them).

In the domain of image recognition (and similarly for speech-to-text), the models are typically trained on a set of images containing a large majority of white persons; thus the models end up being much more performant at recognizing and analyzing light skin–tone faces than darker ones. In those cases, the selection of the training images does play an important role in the biased behavior of the models. That selection is the responsibility of the engineers who design the models — engineers who remain, in large part, white males.

Note also that psychological research indicates that humans recognize faces of their own race more accurately than faces of other races. In 2011, researchers compared two sets of facial recognition solutions, one from Western countries and one from East Asian countries. Their results showed that facial recognition algorithms also struggle with this "other-race effect," with each set of algorithms recognizing local faces more accurately.[2]

In NLP, one of the culprits appears to be the underlying representation of words (word embeddings). Although those models are often trained on relatively generic and representative corpora such as Wikipedia, they nonetheless subsume the existing biases of society that are still implicitly present in our language. Indeed, social science studies have long investigated how gender ideology is embedded in text. One example among many pertains to the presence of women in text. An analysis of business literature reports, for instance, that mentions of men occurred over 100 times more often than mentions of women.[3] Therefore, this latter example demonstrates not so much a problem of bias in the selection of the training data, but rather the problem of bias in society, which is simply captured by the model-training process.

In a nutshell, algorithms are only as good as the data on which they are trained! Humans are hardwired for bias, be it conscious or unconscious. Those cognitive biases are deeply rooted into virtually every aspect of our economic and social environment: workplace, healthcare, scholarship, law enforcement, and marketing, among others. It is therefore no surprise that bias also infiltrates every byte of the data our society produces and, consequently, the algorithms trained on this data.

Thus, the more we are using algorithms and incorporating them into decision-making processes, the more they propagate — if not amplify — our implicit social and cognitive biases, even when we as a society are actively working to eliminate them.

So What Can We Do About It?

There already exists a variety of technical approaches designed to alleviate bias in AI models. The proposed solutions are typically specific to a certain domain or certain kinds of models.

However, a simple first step would be to ensure there is proper human oversight by raising awareness and training people on the importance of identifying and mitigating bias when building models that include variables that may lead to discriminatory decisions. Data scientists (but also the business product owners of the models being developed) should thus determine whether the context of the use of the model and the data that it uses as input could potentially lead to biased decisions. One important measure is to address the problem of diversity in the workplace as a way to ensure the inclusion of a range of critical perspectives in the development of the models.

If there is a risk of developing a biased model, care should be taken to ensure that the decisions made by the model are explicitly independent of the protected variables. In addition, implicit bias in data should be checked at multiple steps of model development:

1. In the input data
2. After data cleaning
3. In the output data
4. During production

Note that in such efforts, the use of interpretable models or the addition of an interpretable layer can be useful as a way to help data scientists analyze the logic of the model they have built. Other approaches involve testing statistical independence between the decision and the sensitive variable.
One practical limitation in all those cases is that checking implicit bias entails having access to the required information. This is a key point. We cannot assess and address bias if we cannot access the necessary inputs. As illustrated by the Apple Card case, imposing blindness to something as critical as gender only makes it harder for a company to detect, prevent, and reverse bias on exactly that variable.

Another challenge is that there are various interpretations of fairness. For instance, group fairness stipulates that subjects in protected and unprotected groups have equal probability of being assigned to the positive class. Another definition of fairness seeks to ensure that both groups have the same positive predicted value (precision).

The AI community is actively investigating ways to measure and address bias, though some of those are model-specific. For instance, to measure the degree of bias present in word-embedding models, researchers in the NLP domain have developed a Word Embedding Association Test inspired by the Implicit Association Test from psychology, which is a standard approach to measuring subconscious bias in humans. If one has a choice between several embedding models, then the results can serve as a selection criterion. When dealing with structured data, researchers from Carnegie Mellon University have proposed a method to alleviate bias generated by the imbalance in the number of features positively correlated with one class, which can lead to biased output even though the training data is unbiased.

In the end, debiasing approaches, whichever ones are used, will necessarily be constraints on models and consequently may lead to a decrease in the models' raw performance. Such a tradeoff is not new in itself, but it should be acknowledged and — more importantly — accepted.

Humans must tell AI what they consider suitable, teach it which information is relevant, and indicate that the outcomes they consider best — ethically, legally, and financially — are those that are free from bias, conscious or otherwise. That is the only way AI can help us create systems that are fairer, more productive, and ultimately better for both business and the broader society.

An Ethical Dimension

All through this discussion, we have purposely avoided implying that all biases observed directly or indirectly in data sets used to train AI models should be removed. Our current perspective is that they should be identified and understood. However, the decision to modify input data to remove one observed bias is not to be taken systemically or automatically. The decision to constrain models with fairness measures seems more straightforward, but it entails the choice of the appropriate definition of fairness, which may not be so simple.

Bias is ingrained in our society, evolving with the way society evolves. As such, algorithmic bias and data bias represent significant challenges for the same reasons cognitive bias and cultural bias are significant challenges for societies. There is no magic wand capable of enabling us to identify and remove all bias from our algorithms and from the data sets we use to train them. Instead, we must take a proactive approach to detecting and understanding biases, evaluating and questioning their impacts, and striving to minimize their negative externalities.

From a social science perspective, the fact that AI models pick up those societal biases is somehow fruitful in itself, providing a way to detect, measure, and understand the evolution of society over time, including its progress.

One final question: As AI can process huge volumes of information, could it be taught to filter out our prejudices as well?

Rim Tehraoui is currently chief data officer of BNP Paribas Group, where she is responsible for developing and implementing the bank's data strategy, making data actionable, and driving analytics, digital transformation, and positive business impact.

Before that, she headed the Risk Anticipation department within BNP Paribas, providing expertise in a forward-looking mode on various risk dimensions to enhance risk anticipation and/or support the bank's development plans. She also established the artificial intelligence practice within the risk function and has been leading the development and the deployment of a comprehensive environmental, social, and governance (ESG) risk management framework, a responsibility that she is still carrying out in her current capacity along with the deployment of an ESG data supply chain.

Prior to that, Rim served at various front-office and strategy positions, developing specific expertise in structuring, investment and portfolio management, capital optimization, funding, and treasury management. She is an alumna of ENSAE Paris Tech and Sciences Po Paris.

Léa Deleris is currently head of the Artificial Intelligence Research team within BNP Paribas RISK Group, which she joined in October 2018. Prior to joining the banking industry, Léa worked at IBM Research, spending four years at IBM Watson Research Center, the company's main research laboratory near New York, and then another eight years managing a team of researchers in artificial intelligence and natural language processing in the IBM Research–Dublin lab in Ireland.

As a researcher, she has investigated a variety of applied and formal problems in the domain of artificial intelligence and risk modeling broadly defined, ranging from vulnerability modeling in eldercare to leveraging knowledge within academic publications to better understand breast cancer risk to contributing to the IBM Debater project, the objective of which is to teach a machine the art of debate.

At BNPP, her team of data scientists is currently working on a wide array of problems linking data, AI, and risk management. Examples include text classification of operational incidents, recommendations for proactive commercial action for leasing, targeted sentiment analysis for risk anticipation, and use of machine learning to alleviate data quality challenges. Léa is an alumna of Ecole Polytechnique. She holds an MS and a PhD from Stanford University.

References

[1]Andrews, Edmund L. "Stanford Researchers Find That Automated Speech Recognition Is More Likely to Misinterpret Black Speakers." *Stanford News*, 23 March 2020 (https://diversityworks.stanford.edu/news/stanford-researchers-find-automated-speech-recognition-more-likely-misinterpret-black-speakers).

[2]Phillips, P. Jonathon, et al. "An Other-Race Effect for Face Recognition Algorithms." *ACM Transactions on Applied Perception*, Vol. 8, No. 2, January 2011 (https://dl.acm.org/doi/10.1145/1870076.1870082).

[3]Fuertes-Olivera, Pedro A. "A Corpus-Based View of Lexical Gender in Written Business English." *English for Specific Purposes*, Vol. 26, No. 2, 2007 (https://www.sciencedirect.com/science/article/abs/pii/S0889490606000330#!).

Magdalena Kortas
Data Scientist
Women in Machine Learning & Data Science

Why Diversity in AI Matters (and Why It's Not about "Political Correctness")

I cannot even count how many times I have heard someone say that diversity in the field of artificial intelligence does not make sense and that companies should just hire the best professionals in the field and put the "diversity" term on a shelf with all the other corporate bullshit phrases. Diversity looks nice in a PowerPoint presentation, they say, but it's very hard to achieve — and why should we?

A Tale of Two Queues

Let us compare an AI algorithm to a toilet.

A toilet.

Imagine you are going to the toilet in a restaurant, or in a cinema, or at the airport, or any other public place. What do you see? There is always a huge queue to the women's restroom, while to the men's, there is usually none. Why? The number of toilet stalls is equal. What is more, the latest UN figures show that the number of women and men is almost equal. For every 100 females, there are 101.8 males. Why does it happen, then?

It's not about women being sluggish. But it is about the need to design unbiased solutions by a diverse group of people.

Why do women wait in queues? There are many reasons why. For 25% of the time, women of reproductive age have their monthly periods, which require more and lengthier toilet visits. Women are usually those who take care of kids and help them with their hygienic activities. Women live longer, so the majority of old people are also women — who may require more (and more frequent) toilet visits. Finally, in the men's room, there can be more urinals, as it requires less space to build them. And it obviously requires less time to use them too.

An equal number of toilets for men and women seems nondiscriminatory, unbiased, and neutral. It seems fair, and it was probably intended to be fair by those who designed it (and probably never waited in a restroom queue). Yet the resulting difference in queue length is patently unfair.

Well-Functioning Algorithms Require Diversity

AI algorithms are only as good as we design them to be and as good as the data we provide them to learn. This is why diversity matters. Without it, algorithms can be:

- Racist. Certain predictive policing algorithms have been shown to per-petuate systemic racism, while some U.S. healthcare allocation algorithms have suggested that Black patients should receive a lower standard of care.
- Sexist. For example, an Amazon recruitment tool showed bias against women, while Facebook's ad algorithm promoted jobs like nursing or secretarial work mostly to women.
- Used to discriminate according to gender. Algorithms might use pro-grammed gender verifications methods, such as an Australian app called "Giggle" that used AI to verify whether the user was a girl.

AI is not racist, sexist, or discriminatory on its own. It is the developers and designers who make it biased, even if that is not their goal. They may simply not be aware of the many ways bias can creep in or may not consider the nuances of social contexts. Building a more diverse team of creators of those algorithms is thus a necessity, not just another example of political correctness.

Political correctness, as commonly understood in public discourse, can consist in avoiding the use of offensive words and phrases and replacing them with more neutral expressions. It can also include self-limitation in the use of symbols and terms that may exclude, marginalize, or offend social groups that experience discrimination. Diversity in AI means more efficient, unbiased, and more accurate algorithms and solutions. It is a benefit, not a limitation.

But diversity can also be misinterpreted. What is more diverse? A group of racially diverse Stanford-taught Americans from wealthy families working in Silicon Valley? Or a group of white men from different backgrounds and continents?

If the group is homogeneous, we are going to have AI that is designed by and works well for that specific group of people. So, the answer is: the more diverse the team, the better, but we need to consider the problem we are working on.

Improving Diversity in AI

Diversity in AI is improving, thanks to the activity of nonprofit, international organizations like Women in Machine Learning & Data Science (WiMLDS) and Women in AI, among others. Bottom-up movements like Omdena bring together people from all over the world, from many backgrounds, to work voluntarily on AI for Good projects. Wide access to free online machine learning courses also supports democratization of AI and diversity in the field (at least for those who have access to the internet and intermediate English language skills).

According to research, women constitute 15%-25% of data science professionals globally.[1] In the city where I grew up, on the Polish coast of the Baltic Sea, female data scientists account for 27% of the local data science workforce.[2] Even if that figure is higher than the world average, there is still a lot to be done.

Members of a local WiMLDS chapter in Gdańsk, Poland

Promoting diversity in an AI team may seem to be just another corporate fad or "political correctness craze," but it is neither of them. In fact, it is a strategy that benefits all of us — the AI algorithm creators as well as the final users. As data scientists, machine learning engineers, AI specialists, or AI team managers, we hold huge responsibility for the influence of the AI we build on people's lives. And with the fast-growing popularity of AI, we will more and more often be in the position of end user ourselves, even if we do not realize it. Then, we may personally bear the consequences of the biased solutions that someone — even in good faith — has created. For example, by waiting in a longer queue to a restroom.

Magdalena Kortas is a data scientist at PredictX in Gdańsk, Poland. She is the co-founder of Women in Machine Learning and Data Science (WiMLDS) Trójmiasto, a machine learning engineer for AI for Good, and a data storytelling enthusiast.

References

[1]Matthews, Kayla. "The Growing Participation of Women in the Data Science Community." KDnuggets, n.d.

[2]Kortas, Magdalena. Analysis of LinkedIn data (https://www.linkedin.com/feed/update/urn:li:activity:6684543928399667201/).

Sonia Ingram
Data Scientist
BJSS

Ethical Data Science: A Checklist of Considerations. Why Should We Care?

Algorithms are impacting more and more aspects of our everyday lives: we need to ensure they are beneficial, not detrimental, to society.

A key challenge within data science and machine learning is that it's such a fast-moving field, completely at odds with governance and legislation. The ethical boundary of how data and tech should be used is therefore often discovered too late by innovative companies inadvertently crossing that line. Furthermore, enforcing governance is complex; algorithms are often highly guarded intellectual property, so governing their use from the outside is nearly impossible.

There have been calls by tech ethicists, such as Cathy O'Neil in her book *Weapons of Math Destruction* (a highly recommended read!), to have a "Hippocratic Oath" for data scientists, to swear to act ethically and do no harm with their models. However, one issue with this approach is that the majority of data scientists have no intention of their algorithms inflicting harm or discriminating in the first place. These algorithms' harmful qualities result from (sometimes huge) oversights. What, then, can data scientists do to build ethical data science solutions?

Points to Consider

Overall Purpose

O'Neil defines a "weapon of math destruction" as an opaque (black-box) algorithm with the potential for large scalability and the ability to cause damage, directly or indirectly. These, then, are the types of use cases where data scientists need to be particularly vigilant to avoid harm.

There are a few questions I find useful when confronted with a new data science problem. Firstly, is a data science solution appropriate for this problem? Using an algorithm or predictive analytics for sensitive use cases, such as predicting children at risk of harm, could be highly detrimental for situations that are missed by the algorithm (false negatives) or wrongly flagged by the algorithm (false positives). For these kinds of situations, use of a data science solution needs to be considered very carefully before such a solution is implemented.

Second, what is the overall aim of the model, and could that in any way cause detriment? Many algorithms directly impact individuals, such as those that decide exam grades or loan approvals. What are the consequences of the algorithm getting it wrong? Others can have a more indirect impact on individuals. For example, algorithms that advise students on potential careers wouldn't directly impact the student's life, but the wrong advice could cause them to question their self-worth or make them feel their desired career is unattainable.

If a detrimental outcome is identified, could the problem be repositioned to benefit society instead? For example, say an algorithm is being developed to predict the likelihood of a person released on bail to re-offend. Could it instead be repositioned to predict the people most likely to need additional support following their release?

Solution Design

Once the purpose has been confirmed, it's time to think about how the solution will be implemented. First, is it going to provide decision support and require a human in the loop who ultimately decides whether or not the model's prediction is appropriate? If so, what is the risk of automation bias (the difficulty humans have with refuting automated recommendations)?

Furthermore, is the solution going to build on human strengths or play to our weaknesses? For example, driverless cars require passengers to remain vigilant and poised to take control whenever needed, but this kind of monotonous situation is exactly what causes humans to become bored and lose concentration. What is the definition of good performance for this use case? Is it more important to minimize false positive predictions or false negatives, and what are the consequences of each? If the solution is fully automated, who is ultimately responsible for its predictions? Who can people affected by it complain or appeal to?

Transparency and Explainability

In the summer of 2020, as a result of the Covid-19 pandemic, the U.K. Office of Qualifications and Examinations Regulation (Ofqual) used an algorithm to determine A-level results for students in lieu of their taking exams. The algorithm came under intense criticism due to discrimination claims, but what was unusual about it was the 318-page report on the algorithm and how it worked, which was published shortly after its results were published. Had this report been published prior to the publication of results, or had development of the algorithm been more collaborative, it is likely that its faults would have been rectified early, and it would not have been scrapped in favor of using teachers' predicted grades.

With machine learning, it's not just the algorithm that determines how it works, but also the data it was trained on. Although legislation such as GDPR and The Filter Bubble Transparency Act call for companies to make clear to users how their data is being used and to offer them more control, transparency of algorithms themselves is essential for building trustable AI solutions and trust in AI solutions.

Explainability is another important tool to this end. The ability to explain to a customer why their loan has been refused by an algorithm and what they can do to improve their chances of success for a subsequent application is the most fundamental aspect of explainability. However, different levels of explainability can be required for different stakeholders, an issue the Bank of England has proposed a framework to address.

Data Validity

Where data is used to train models, good-quality, representative data is essential. There are so many examples of algorithms being trained on biased data and becoming biased as a result: from facial recognition algorithms not being trained on diverse faces to résumé-screening models being trained on historical, biased data sets. Using data representative of the population who will be impacted by the algorithm is key, as is regularly checking for data creep, which could require model retraining.

Furthermore, it is important to properly explore data with regard to majority and minority groups within the dataset. Are minority groups appropriately represented or missing altogether? If the latter, is there a reason for this (e.g., were some groups historically unable to contribute to this data?) and can it be rectified? If not, should minority groups be oversampled or assigned higher weightings to counter this deficiency?

Proxies

Including sensitive data such as gender or ethnicity in training data for machine learning models can cause fear in data scientists, as they worry that this may cause their models to become biased. However, by excluding this data, models can still become biased — just without giving data scientists the means to check whether this is the case! Biases could stem from the inclusion of proxies to sensitive features; that is, features that are closely linked to sensitive features but are not sensitive themselves, such as salary and its link with gender. It is therefore best to check for correlations between all features with sensitive features before relying on one of these potentially biased features in your model.

Another issue with proxies relates to trying to predict one. For example, if you want to model teacher performance, there's no great single measure of what makes a good teacher. Instead, proxies such as student grades would need to be used, which may not directly correlate with the desired outcome of performance. After all, a great teacher may not have the brightest or best-prepared students, while a poor teacher could engage in grade inflation. Use of proxies should therefore be approached with caution.

Fairness

Stratifying predictions by groups (gender, ethnicity, etc.) to check for differences in outcomes between them is the simplest way to investigate fairness. Differences in prediction accuracy between groups should also be checked. This was one flaw of the U.K. grading algorithm. When predicting grades for the previous year, the algorithm was only 40% accurate for some subjects, yet it was implemented across all subjects.

Likewise, had results from facial recognition models been stratified by gender and ethnicity before going live, biases could have been identified by the companies developing them.

If bias is detected between groups in binary classification models, and this can't be rectified by improving training data or reweighting groups, algorithmic fairness can be enforced whereby the proportions of true and false positive predictions are restricted between groups (see an in-depth explanation here[1]).

User Testing

Too many AI flaws were only discovered after a product had gone live, yet they should have been picked up during user testing. Facial recognition biases are a major example of this. Had diverse teams representative of end users been used to test the algorithms, it is likely that the gulf in performance would have been found earlier.

In Summary

This is not an exhaustive checklist to ensure ethical AI, and development of solid governance for the field remains crucial. However, until such governance is in place, it depends on the people designing, developing, implementing, and testing these solutions to ensure they are fit for purpose, non-discriminatory, and beneficial to society.

It's up to us.

Sonia Ingram is a data scientist working at BJSS. After obtaining a PhD in molecular biology, Sonia decided to move into the world of data science and has since worked on projects in healthcare and finance. She is an avid proponent of AI ethics and the societal benefits that can be achieved with AI.

Reference

[1]Cortez, Valeria. "How to Define Fairness to Detect and Prevent Discriminatory Outcomes in Machine Learning." *Towards Data Science*, 23 September 2019 *(https://towardsdatascience.com/how-to-define-fairness-to-detect-and-prevent-discriminatory-outcomes-in-machine-learning-ef23fd408ef2).*

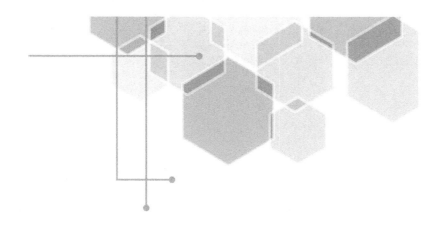

DATA AVAILABILITY

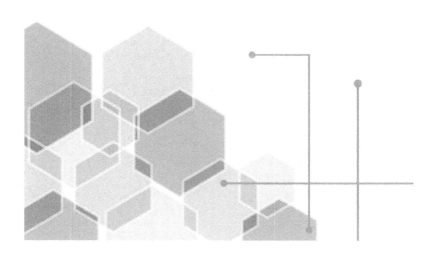

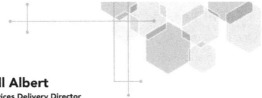

Merrill Albert
Data Services Delivery Director
Trellance

What the 2020 Census Tells Us About Data Management

I call myself a "data person." Professionally, my data career started with a bachelor of mathematics degree from the University of Waterloo, and I have worked with data ever since.

I was probably born this way. I see statistics in the news and question whether the data they used was appropriate. Data is what it's all about. When you can't trust your data, you can't trust the analytics generated from that data. Worse, you could be gleaning what you think are amazing insights, only to discover later that these were based on flawed data. That could lead to bad business decisions and/or public embarrassment.

How do you get your data right, and how do you define "right"? You need to prevent problems from getting into your data. If problems do creep in, you need to fix them as early as possible. The longer you leave problems in your databases, the more time and money it will take to fix all the areas the data has permeated.

I work in the field of data management, which is a discipline in and of itself. Through careful management, decision-making, business rules, and implementation, we take care of data.

But explaining data to people can be difficult. Unless you can tell a story with it, data can sound too theoretical. When I considered what I was going to say in this essay, a story fell into my lap — or rather, my mailbox. This is the story of the 2020 U.S. census.

A Tale of Two Addresses

One day, I received my census form and filled it out online. Six weeks later, I received another census form. I took a closer look.

Every census address has a unique ID, and this form had a different ID from the earlier one. It was my address, but it was slightly different. One of the words in my address is "Captain," and one of the versions had abbreviated it as "Cpt." I live in a metropolitan area that has two valid city names, and these forms varied in that respect too. Although different, they were both valid addresses for me.

Throughout my career, I've seen so many companies struggle to reconcile addresses. It shouldn't be that way. The USPS publishes standard abbreviations. Software is available to automate the standardization, such as turning "Captain" into "Capt." The Census Bureau doesn't seem to have done this.

Some people might think this isn't a big deal. "So you got two census forms in the mail. Toss one out," you say. But wait — this error has implications. The U.S. government uses census information to determine the number of seats in Congress. They use it to determine funding for schools, roads, and public services. Family history researchers will use it (in 72 years). I'm sure I'm not the only person who received multiple forms, but we don't know the magnitude of the problem. It may not be significant, but we won't know unless we look further.

A Human Problem

What went wrong? Many people will blame it on a "computer problem." That's not it. The computer didn't cause the problem. A human caused the problem. We just don't know which human.

When we follow good data management practices, one thing we talk about is "data governance." When we're properly governing our data, we know where the decision rights lie. People throughout the organization collectively use their knowledge to make decisions. What happened here?

Perhaps lists of addresses came from multiple sources that had to be reconciled into a single list. To do that, you define business rules to bring those addresses together. You need to know that "Captain" and "Cpt." are the same. You need to know that two city names (e.g., "Manhattan" and "New York City") are referring to the same place. In data management, we refer to this as "master data management." We want to get to a "single source of the truth."

In the case of the census, were the business rules properly governed so the right people made the decisions? Were the business rules shared with the programmers and tested to demonstrate that they were programmed correctly? These are problems caused by people, not computers.

The Ramifications of Bad Data

Data quality is a huge part of data management, and we need high-quality data for the census. Before anything is released into production, it must be tested. Many organizations don't give the care they should to testing. If Census Bureau employees had properly tested the business rules, data, and programs before sending the census forms, they would have found the error that showed up in my mailbox. Census officials could have stopped it earlier when it was cheaper to fix. The code could have been reprogrammed, retested, validated, and then sent. Doing all this could have delayed the census, but it would have been accurate. Now we're dealing with the problem and its implications.

The majority of people who got multiple census forms aren't data people like me. If it happened to you, you might ignore the additional forms. You'll remember that you already completed your form and just throw out the new one.

However, the Census Bureau doesn't recognize it as a duplicate address. Their records show that you didn't fill out your census form. You will continue to be hounded with forms in the mail until they finally send a census worker to your home. Not only have they spent additional money to send you extra forms in the mail, but now they're spending money on census workers. They need census workers in any case, but depending on the magnitude of the problem, they may need to hire more. And since the 2020 census is occurring during a pandemic, it is expected that there will be repeat visits because people don't want to open their doors to strangers.

Another possibility is that you will fill out the second form, having forgotten that you already filled out a first. Perhaps you have multiple people in your home, and you didn't realize that someone else already completed it. The Census Bureau receives that information, and one of two things happens next. If they don't realize that some people got multiple forms, now they are double-counting people. This can easily skew numbers, affecting public services and representation in Congress. If, on the other hand, they realize they're double-counting, they will have to go through the forms and remove the duplicates.

But are they really duplicates? In many cases, they are. Households don't change too quickly, so as long as the forms are filled out accurately, they will match (with the exception of that address problem). The census, however, spans a period of months, so it is possible that people moved, were born, or died during that time. Those two forms for that one address might actually wind up having different results. Does the Census Bureau then try to reconcile them? Or do they just accept the chaos of their results? Applying this concept to your business, you can see how finding a data problem too late in the process is going to cost you time, effort, and money to pull yourself out of the quagmire.

There's yet another option. Ignore the issue. If you have a population of 1,000,000 and send multiple forms to 100 of them, that number might not be significant enough to act on. If multiple forms go to 100,000, that might attract a little more attention.

So you need to understand the implications of bad data. Depending on your needs, you might need perfection in your data. Is it a life-or-death issue?

If you don't require perfection, is there a threshold you'll accept? If the problem extends beyond that threshold, what happens next? If the overall business decision is to move ahead with some bad data, is there a subset of people who will be adversely affected by that decision? If so, will you need to communicate with them?

The Bigger Picture

Being my family's genealogist, I also think ahead to what the data errors in the 2020 census mean. In 72 years, family history researchers will have access to this census data, and they'll be trying to make sense of it. What will they do when they see their ancestors listed multiple times? What are people going to think about the way the 2020 census was conducted? Will people trust it?

What about history? I stumbled across a problem with the 2020 census. Unless the Census Bureau's programs got recoded for 2020, it's highly likely that prior censuses were also wrong. That means decisions the government has made based on prior census data could also be inaccurate. We'll likely never know.

Although I've told a story about data with the 2020 census, all decisions have their own data story. People generate analytics and then derive insights from those analytics, but they have to make sure that there were people taking care of the data first. Without good data, there's no point in continuing with analytics. A well-managed data environment, however, will take you far.

Merrill Albert is a lifelong data person with a combination of industry and consulting experience. She knows both theory and how to apply it. Merrill has lived data problems and knows how to solve them. She believes in understanding the business needs to solve the problem, keeping a tool-agnostic view. Merrill is also passionate about companies having the right high-quality data, used in a compliant manner, to make appropriate and timely decisions. She helps companies better manage their data to drive value from it.

Marion Shaw
Director Data & Analytics
SDL plc

Master Data During Covid-19

Covid-19 has impacted every business across the world in one way or another. People were furloughed, remote working became the norm, and every business changed in order to make the best of the situation. Data became even more important overnight as businesses raced to adapt to the pandemic. Data was everywhere: every country in the world held regular briefings with graphs and numbers, statistics were suddenly at the forefront of the news. People started talking about graphs, R-rates, and daily averages, and all this had the unexpected side effect of increasing data literacy.

Before the Covid-19 pandemic, the data team at the company where I work had already planned to implement a master data initiative on our customer data. Master data initiatives can be prompted by a variety of factors. Consider this common scenario:

- A company has multiple systems containing customer data.
- Accrued over time through acquisition, each system has an important role in the day-to-day operation of the company.
- Each is governed by a different part of the business, with its own rules and processes.
- Some of the systems are connected for functional reasons and exchange data on a regular basis.
- Data maturity is low; there are no data lineage diagrams.
- The appetite for consolidated data is high, and a data-driven culture is developing faster than the technology supporting it. (This is a good position to be in, as everyone understands the value of data.)

We decided to start our master data effort with customer data, as this was in line with our business strategy. Ensuring customer satisfaction is at the core of our company ethos.

Given the complexity of our customer data and the number of intersecting data points, this project was not going to be easy. We decided to approach this undertaking the same way you would eat an elephant — one bite at a time!

Standardization

The first task was to see whether we could standardize customer names across systems and map them together. So how do you do that?

We started by talking to each part of the business and determining the key attributes each department and business unit required of customer data in order to operate efficiently. Each of the business units had different key attributes that were important to them. Few of them needed to consider attributes in other parts of the business; they operated in silos on a need-to-know basis. While this worked efficiently for the operation of the business, it made it challenging to see the full 360-degree view of each of our customers and to predict the right actions to increase satisfaction.

The Golden Record

Once we gathered the information from the business, we mapped the key attributes to discover that no single system held all the key attributes. In order to create a truly comprehensive view of our customers, we needed to consolidate all of these attributes into a Golden Record.[1]

---

[1]"The Golden Record is the ultimate prize in the data world. A fundamental concept within Master Data Management (MDM) defined as the single source of truth; one data point that captures all the necessary information we need to know about a member, a resource, or an item in our catalogue — assumed to be 100% accurate."
(Source: DataClarity UK)

In a break with best practice, we decided to create the Golden Record in the analytical data warehouse instead of designating a source system. This was in order to get the job done faster and to ensure that the Golden Record would be on a merged basis with all the attributes in a single place — our single source of truth.

We would then use the high-quality consolidated data in the Common Data Model in the future to populate any new systems implemented to ensure high-quality data is propagated back into the ecosystem.

This is the model we created (see Figure 1):

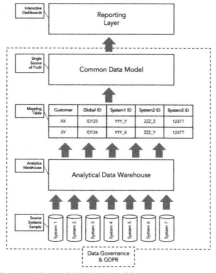

Figure 1 — The model we developed for our customer data project.

Consolidation

The next challenge: how do you consolidate over 24,000 customer records? To be honest, given the disparate datasets and the importance to the business, the answer is "manually."

Where do you find the time to manually map all these records, while also executing business as usual? Good question.

As we launched this project, Covid-19 happened, and the business moved to remote working overnight. Covid-19 significantly impacted the data team, as everyone needed more information, more visibility, and better models to mitigate the impact of Covid-19 on the business.

At this point, the business had a team of facilities people who, due to remote working, had no tasks. The business did not want to furlough these individuals, as they are instrumental to the day-to-day operation of the U.K. offices when open. Instead, we assigned these people to the data team to help with the mapping exercise.

Using an internationally recognized standard, the DUNS number, this team searched each and every record and added this unique identifier to each record, creating a giant mapping table across systems. This enabled our database administrator to create a mapping layer in the data warehouse. This team was instrumental to the customer data project, which would have diverted resources from daily operations had the data team needed to do the mapping. We were able to use human resources that would otherwise have been furloughed to progress and support a core data strategy and provide value to the business.

During the course of this mapping project, we were able to correct inaccurate data, update data to the latest version, consolidate duplicate records, link customer to parent company, and supplement the data with DUNS information to provide a more detailed view of the customer both from internal and external data sources. These were linked to the unique identifier in the customer dataset and the originating systems to knit them all together.

As this work progressed, we started adding the key attributes to our customer master dataset, system by system, to create our customer intelligence dataset and a single source of truth. On top of this, we started building interactive dashboards to give the business a consolidated view and knowledge. As more data is linked together, the value exponentially increases, and more knowledge and wisdom are extracted.

The analytical data warehouse remains the single source of truth and a consolidated view of customer data. Around this model, we implemented data governance and data quality checks at each point of ingestion to ensure high-quality data remains in the Golden Record. Data stewards were nominated in each system and made responsible for ensuring the continued quality of data entering their system and traveling through the system. A minimum level of data was required in order to add a new customer to the ecosystem.

Conclusion

Our customer data initiative has been an unqualified success. It demonstrates that — even during the most challenging time — with planning, cooperation, and hard work, value can be extracted from data.

Marion Shaw is a data professional who is passionate about data; she has two daughters and a fluffy dog. Originally from Ireland, Marion now lives in Bracknell, just outside London.

She is a Six Sigma Black Belt, data modeler, and dashboard designer, as well as an advocate for Women in Data. She wants all women and girls to believe in themselves and shoot for the moon. As far as she is concerned, women have everything they need inside them to succeed — they just need to believe in themselves.

Valerie Logan
CEO & Founder
The Data Lodge, Inc.

Debunking the Top 5 Myths About Data Literacy

With the emergence of any new concept or idea in the market, such as data literacy, there is often a frenzy of confusion, misconceptions, and noise that follows. While this frenzy is often the product of good intentions, nonetheless it does not help the collective cause of creating clarity and alignment and getting started productively.

With data literacy programs becoming the hottest topic among chief data officer types, in the pursuit of fostering the ever-elusive data-informed culture, three questions surface regularly:

- What is data literacy, really?
- What is a data literacy program?
- And what is it not?

Let's unpack the answers.

As a bit of context, let's start with a simple definition of what data literacy is and what makes up a healthy data literacy program.

> *Data literacy* is the ability to read, write, and communicate with data in context, in both work and life. It is based upon nurturing both shared language (vocabulary) and modern skills for thinking, engaging, and applying data for impact. (Source: The Data Lodge, Inc.)

A data literacy program is the intentional commitment to upskill the workforce and culture, unlocking the full potential of all associates with the language and skills needed to leverage data and insights at the moments that matter most, with a blend of engagement, development, and enablement activities. (Source: The Data Lodge, Inc.)

So where does the confusion come in? Let's explore the top five myths about data literacy, followed by three ways you can actively debunk them.

Exploring the Data Literacy Myths

Data Literacy Myth #1: Data literacy = training.
It's true...
Upskilling the workforce with targeted skills assessment and development efforts is indeed foundational to data literacy, and training is key (both self-paced and prescribed).

But...
Data literacy programs must include and provide more than "just" training! Instead, they should include a wide array of development activities and change management mechanisms: coaching, language development, community development, supporting resources, technology enablement, as well as bottom-up culture hacks and support.

Data Literacy Myth #2: Data literacy is about internal structured data and statistics.
It's true...
Analysis of internal structured data is critical for key performance measurement, monitoring, and business improvement.

But...
Data literacy programs must reflect the wide and ever-changing diversity of data sources and analytical methods available today. We must foster an appreciation of the diversity of data (internal/external, varying data types and

latencies) and the wide variety of methods for analyzing and synthesizing content.

Data Literacy Myth #3: Data literacy = data visualization and storytelling.
It's true...
Business intelligence self-service tools, data visualization capabilities, and the focus on the art (and science) of powerful storytelling have been vital drivers of the data literacy movement and demonstrating the power of data.

But...
Data literacy must not stop there! It must also serve as a basis for understanding data quality, ethics, bias, privacy, and the unlocking of collaboration and innovation across an incredibly diverse, talented, and untapped workforce.

Data Literacy Myth #4: Data literacy is about making everyone a junior data scientist.
It's true...
As the future of work emerges, role and skill requirements shift. Ways of working are morphing and becoming more data-driven and analytical in nature.

But...
People are scared. Many are intimidated by concepts such as statistics, math, data, and technology. They hear the term "data literacy" and immediately feel like they will be left behind because they think "I'm not a data person" or "I'm not a math person."

Instead, we can frame data literacy as an appropriate blend of three areas: business acumen, data awareness, and analytical understanding. With this framing, everyone brings something to the data party! Even a front-line retail associate, driver, or call center representative can bring their understanding to the language of data, and that is valuable. From the boardroom to the breakroom, we must clarify that the intention is not for all to become data scientists. It is about helping people to think about, engage with, and apply data for value when and where it matters most in their specific role.

Appreciating the respective roles that all employees play is key, from entering quality data to innovating with data, protecting data, sharing data, and using data ethically.

Data Literacy Myth #5: Data literacy is just a work skill.
It's true...
Data literacy is a critical work and professional skill.

But...
It's also a vital personal life skill. As parents, patients, consumers, and citizens, we all benefit from improved data literacy, which enables us to be discerning consumers of information, make data-informed life decisions, and appreciate and protect our own personal data. Investing in workforce data literacy is a way of giving back to our employees.

Debunking the Data Literacy Myths

What are we to do to mitigate the risks of these misconceptions? It's easier than you may think.

It starts with being on the lookout for them! Then, you can use a few simple techniques to debunk these myths, specifically:

1. Seek first to understand.

Assuming good intentions, it always helps to approach someone (who may be narrowly defining data literacy) by first seeking to clarify their language and context. Recognize that this is still a new and emerging area, and we all come at new areas from our own backgrounds and biases. Stay open.

2. Clarify intention and common ground.

Engaging in futile debates serves no one, although productive debates are always welcome! Enlist and welcome diverse perspectives in the conversation of what data literacy means to the organization and to individuals. Use the improv technique of "Yes, and..." to create shared purpose and intent. With improv techniques, you can support teams in openly sharing their diverse perspectives and building upon a shared view together.

3. Be explicit.

Many disconnects start with generalities and lack of shared context, collectively and personally. Make data literacy personal with words, visuals, and examples. Make it fun. Work top down and bottom up — grass roots. Version, share, and iterate real examples of the needs and drivers that are building your case for data literacy today. Embrace the many ways you can foster and enhance data literacy from the boardroom to the breakroom.

Why Does This Matter?

These data literacy myths, if left to linger unaddressed, can become significant root issues of a problematic and less-than-impactful data literacy program. In many cases, you will have one shot to initiate such a program, and the initial perceptions, clarity, and framing of the needs and drivers will be the strongest predictor of the future success and near-term impact and viability of the program.

When asked how to get started with a data literacy program, the answer is always the same: craft your case for change. Make it clear and compelling and explicitly mitigate these myths.

At the end of the day, data literacy is all about shared language, and that starts with a shared definition and framing of data literacy itself.

Valerie Logan, who founded The Data Lodge in 2019, is as committed to data literacy as it gets. Offering advisory services, bootcamps, and community services, Valerie is certifying the world's first Data Literacy Program Leads across commercial and public sectors. Previously, she was a Gartner VP in data and analytics and a leading advisor to chief data and analytics officers. Valerie pioneered research in data literacy and nurturing the "speaking of data" by creating Information as a Second Language (ISL). In 2018, she received Gartner's Top Thought Leadership Award for her work in data literacy. Valerie has over two decades of global consulting experience and five years in the telecom space at both the field and enterprise levels. In 2018, she was named a finalist in the "Data Leader of the Year" category of the Information Age Women in IT Awards. She was also recognized by Consulting Magazine in 2008 as one of top eight women in global consulting. Valerie holds a BS in mathematics from the SUNY College at Buffalo and an MS in applied mathematics from New Mexico State University with a concentration in operations research. She lives in the Adirondack Mountains with her husband Brian at Brant Lake, New York.

Iria E
Data Engineer | Senior Consultant
Deloitte LLC

Why Big Data Needs an Agile Data Operations (DataOps) Team

Yes, you read the title correctly — I said "DataOps". Just as we have DevOps, we also need DataOps in big data. The Gartner Glossary defines DataOps as "the hub for collecting and distributing data, with a mandate to provide controlled access to systems of record for customer and marketing performance data, while protecting privacy, usage restrictions, and data integrity."

```
def dataOpsContent(self, agile, devOps, leanManufacturing):
    """ What makes up dataOps?"""
    return agile + devOps + leanManufacturing
```

The emphasis on DataOps has grown a lot in the last couple of years. Personally, I have seen more discussions around it from late 2019 into 2020. Already in 2018, Gartner's hype cycle[1] had DataOps on the rise; hence, analytics leaders have to strategize a way to keep up with these emerging data management technologies. We need to deliver quality products at the same rate as data changes to meet customer needs, and DataOps is key in delivering this (see Figure 1).

Figure 1 — Data operations.

Are you thinking about a career path in data? DataOps is another prospect. So if you are already part of an operations team, you most likely have some of the skills required. DataOps is the collaboration piece between the data science team and business stakeholders. The idea is to ensure efficiency in the data lifecycle (DLC), and who better to help achieve that goal than DataOps?

```
def dataOpsSkills(self, interestedInDataOps, haveSkills):
"""Note that the skills for this role depend:
    - Organization
    - Projects
    - Cost e.t.c """
  if interestedInDataOps:
    return haveSkills in ['automation', 'scripting', 'communication', 'customer
support', 'and lots more']
```

You might be wondering, don't I need all of the machine learning, deep learning, and Python that data scientists and data engineers require? Not necessarily. The mistake most companies make is interlocking roles in big data. As essential as it is to collaborate, it's best to leave data engineers or data scientists out of data operations. That way, we can reduce waste during the DLC.

As companies embrace this strategy, most times DataOps tends to overlap with data engineering because of the misconception that it is somewhat DevOps in nature. However, this team role is more about understanding the different facets of a big data team from the code, infrastructure, communication, and — most importantly — data perspectives.

```
def defineAgileDataOps(self, agile, dataOps, devOps):
  """ What is Agile DataOps?"
  If dataOps == devOps:
      return false
```

Agile is one of the key ingredients to a perfect DataOps team. DataOps is more than a data management strategy and best practices. Rather, it incorporates all of the different facets of an Agile big data team.

Applying Agile Principles to Big Data

Many of us are familiar with The Agile Manifesto.[2]:

> We are uncovering better ways of developing software by doing it and helping others do it. Through this work we have come to value:
> *Individuals and interactions* over processes and tools
> *Working software* over comprehensive documentation
> *Customer collaboration* over contract negotiation
> *Responding to change* over following a plan
> That is, while there is value in the items on the right,
> we value the items on the left more"

When we apply these principles to big data, we get the Agile Big Data (ABD) Manifesto:

> We are discovering better ways to manage big data.
> Through this work we have come to value:
> *Individuals and interactions* over processes and tools
> *Clean, quality data* over comprehensive documentation
> *Fair and unbiased user collaboration* over contract negotiation
> *Responding to change in data* over following a plan
> That is, while there is value in the items on the right,
> we value the items on the left more.

Data is ever-changing with technological advancement; thus it is only proper to adopt techniques that can yield the most efficient outcome. Implementing the ABD Manifesto is one basic approach to help avoid some of the main problems that we have seen arise from poor data strategy.

So what is Agile Big Data? ABD could be considered as the foundation of most organizations, especially in the times we are in, with GDPR, the California Consumer Privacy Act, the Brazilian General Data Protection Law, and the many more laws coming up. The Agile framework is considered a value-driven development, so it is only proper to apply it to one's data if the whole idea of having data is to gain insight/value. Every organization can find a way to implement and make ABD work for them.

The idea is to ensure that we are able to adapt along with technological changes and advancement, which is possible as long as we adhere to the ABD goal, which is to provide solutions by analyzing the data properly. As simple as this goal might appear, if the ABD Manifesto is not followed appropriately, then we will have solutions that are biased or just plain wrong.

The ABD Approach

A big data project consists of several different components (see Figure 2). Delivering on these components requires the following:

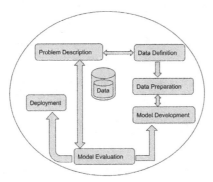

Figure 2 — The data development lifecycle.

An Agile Team

This is the most important part of a data project. I know you'll ask, "What about the data?" Yes, data is vital, but how can you truly get value from it without the work of a diverse team? You need the right blend of expertise, experience, and curiosity, which is the most important thing to have. Such a team will able to implement a mixture of the different Lean-Agile and project management frameworks. Diverse team members will bring their unique perspective and ideas, which have been molded by the team's culture, experience, and environment. With this diversity, there is the possibility of producing an unbiased solution.

Data-Driven Development

Is it possible to consider data-driven development (DDD) as an Agile framework? Data-driven development is intertwined with a test-driven development approach and rests on an automation foundation. There might not be a standard definition for DDD, but I want to think of it as data-centric development, where the final system outcome is based on the data to ensure the final result is unbiased and valuable. In order to ensure an accepted final result, we must take into consideration the quality of the data, business models, and rules, all of which I believe are built from a solid team.

Conclusion

Operations are vital to every organization, especially when you have a diverse team of people working to solve a complex problem. To really answer the question we asked at the beginning — "What is Agile Big Data?" — I want to think of it as data itself, combined with the Agile principles and technologies needed to develop applications that are useful to the end users, applications that help solve the problem objective for which they were created. I think all of this can be achieved with an Agile DataOps team.

Iria E is a data engineer who is passionate about big data. She started a blog, @bigdataprincess, to share data skills and resources and to serve as a platform for gaining innovative skills to apply to the data challenges we face today. When not talking data, Iria loves gardening, going for walks, and reading.

References

[1]Panetta, Kasey. "5 Trends Emerge in the Gartner Hype Cycle for Emerging Technologies, 2018." Gartner, 16 August 2018 (www.gartner.com/smarterwithgartner/5-trends-emerge-in-gartner-hype-cycle-for-emerging-technologies-2018/).

[2]The Agile Manifesto (www.agilemanifesto.org).

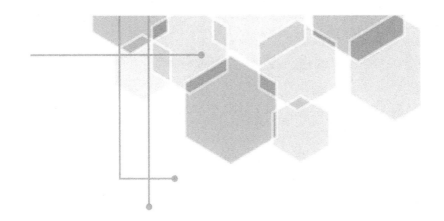

MODEL PREPARATION

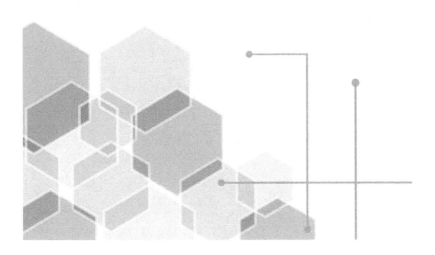

Mai Alowaish
Chief Data Officer
Gulf Bank

Understanding the User Journey with Event-Based Models in Digital Analytics

*"Every trackable interaction creates a data point,
and every data point tells a piece of the customer's story."*
Paul Roetzer,
Founder and CEO
Marketing Artificial Intelligence Institute

The customer journey is no longer a straight path. The proliferation of innovative new platforms and devices has fundamentally altered customer behaviors and preferences. Marketers have been forced to implement omnichannel marketing campaigns to reach the right customer, at the right time, and on the right channel.

Omnichannel marketing has likewise fundamentally altered the role of the data analyst. The modern analyst serves as a storyteller of sorts, attempting to weave together disparate data sources to glean a comprehensive and meaningful understanding of the customer journey.

Analysts accomplish this by looking closely at the conversion process to gauge the effectiveness of their marketing campaigns. Each platform offers unique dimensions and metrics. Yet conversion goals are largely the same across all devices — for instance, motivating a customer to sign up for a newsletter or to make a purchase. By combining data on user actions and conversions across platforms, analysts can identify the most effective marketing strategies.

For example, consider the following customer journey. A customer views a promotion on a social media platform. He opts in to a newsletter to receive a 20% off coupon. The coupon is viewed on a mobile device and a product added to his shopping cart. The cart is abandoned, but a purchase is subsequently made through a retargeting advertisement on a PC (see Figure 1). The one constant here is the user, which aptly becomes the basic unit of measurement. So analysts examine the user and the actions he took along the way, regardless of the platform or device used.

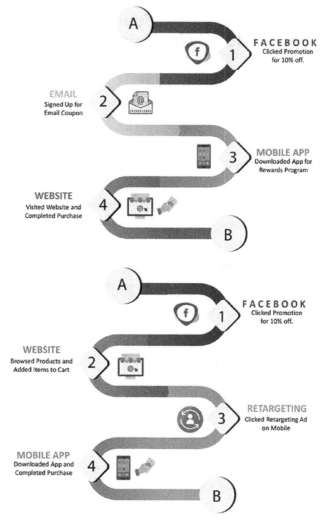

Figure 1 — Different user paths to conversion.

Event-Based Models and Omnichannel User Behavior

Event-based models produce analyzable data by merging device and platform data together. This data is easy to query and can be used to better understand user behavior. Event-based models require that user actions follow the same architecture regardless of the device or platform used. User actions are tracked, and meaning is added through analysis.

Let's return to our example from above. Recall that our customer added a product to his shopping cart on his mobile device. While the cart was subsequently abandoned, this "Add to cart" event can serve as an indication of the customer's interest in that particular product or category (when studying interests and segmenting users). This same event can also be the first step in a sales funnel (when studying checkout behavior). Thus, event data can vary based on the action that is being tracked.

Event-based models are not just about collecting more data about user actions. Rather, analysts must seamlessly integrate data from multiple sources and know how to use that data to gain a macro-level view of the customer journey. Armed with that understanding, analysts must use the right tools to provide compelling user experiences at the right moments.

It is important not to lose sight of the forest for the trees. Focusing on isolated occurrences or performance metrics provides an incomplete understanding. Marketers must focus on the user rather than the platform or device. To be successful, businesses should switch to user-centric analytical mindsets before transitioning to event-based data sets. According to an IBM white paper, "The unified tracking models allowed us to convert these events into behaviors and tie the behaviors to individuals using a 'single identity' model. The data across web, mobile, email, social, and other channels is not siloed anymore."[1]

Successful marketers get to know their customers and seek to build long-term relationships. Demographics and psychographics do little to help marketers predict customer behavior. Past customer actions tell us more about what they are likely to do in the future. For instance, adding an item to a shopping cart tells us more about a customer's interests than does his or her age group or geographic location. The key to knowing customers and developing meaningful relationships is understanding their actions across channels and giving them what they need without them having to ask.

By simplifying data collection, event-based models help marketers to seamlessly analyze data at the macro level. Unified customer data and technologies like machine learning tools and predictive analytics help to develop actionable insights. For example, consider a user who downloads the Amazon app on her mobile phone, searches for products on the Amazon website using her PC, and watches videos on Prime Video.

In the past, collecting and integrating data from these devices to build customer profiles was a time-consuming and arduous task, with important data often lost in transition. Delays prevented marketers from taking meaningful action. With event-based models, common events are tracked across platforms and devices, giving marketers actionable insights in real time.

For example, a customer who viewed similar products on different devices may be provided with new product recommendations based on her interests. Marketers can leverage artificial intelligence and machine learning technologies to sort through user data to gain powerful insights to drive personalized and high-converting customer experiences.

More Data = Improved Customer Insights and Relationships

In 2018, the *MIT Sloan Management Review* published a report that examined the use of analytics to improve customer engagement.[2] The authors discussed how analysts can utilize multiple data sources to develop customer insights and strengthen relationships with customers. The report essentially concludes that collecting more data leads to more valuable and actionable insights.

More than just collecting data, however, marketers need to be able to act on the data in real time. To do this, users must be connected across devices through data-driven attribution. Analysts collect user-level data on micro conversions that lead to macro conversions or predefined business objectives.

This data is used to understand how customers navigate across various touch-points as they progress through the user journey. Marketers are tasked with anticipating needs, expectations, and desires at each touchpoint.

Anonymous customer data presents unique challenges. Collecting anony-mous data sources across platforms and devices leads to large volumes of aggregated data. When this data is integrated with data from traditional marketing channels, the resulting dataset becomes a candidate for another analysis model, such as media mix modeling.

Using media mix modeling, marketers can measure the effect of different elements as well as how each element contributed to the overall objective. Media mix modeling can provide higher-level insights than data-driven attri-bution models due to the inclusion of traditional marketing channels.

Event-based data models play an integral role in integrating all data sources into one place to provide actionable insights in real time.

Start Small and Apply What You Learn

Integrating data sources and changing data models can be challenging. For newcomers, the best approach is to start small. For instance, start by connecting web and app analytics. Learn as you go. Apply what you learn to improve your methods. Think about other ways that customers engage with the business. Gradually integrate data from these other channels.

Focus on structuring tracking around the user. Collect and analyze data across the entire user journey. Integrate data sources from different platforms and devices to gain a unified view of the user. By combining data, marketers gain a higher-level understanding of the achievement of their overall business objec-tives rather than being limited to gauging the success of a specific platform.

As Forrester consultants Nick Phelps and Sophia Christakis observe, "A person-level data approach will help drive marketing excellence. Organizations that use person-level data perform better on their business and marketing goals and show stronger revenue growth than firms who do not."[3]

Mai Alowaish is the chief data officer at Gulf Bank. With experience in e-commerce applications and digital analytics in both the United States and Kuwait, Mai has implemented a variety of analytics and e-commerce solutions and enabled digital transformation for online retailers, financial institutions, airlines, and more. Mai is an active member and mentor with the Digital Analytics Association (DAA) and the recipient of the 2019 DAA President's Award.

References

[1]IBM. "10 Common Barriers to Understanding the Customer Journey and How to Overcome Them." Available at (www3.technologyevaluation.com/research/white-paper/10-common-barriers-to-understanding-the-customer-journey-and-how-to-overcome-them.html), last accessed on 4 January 2021.

[2]Ransbotham, Sam, and David Kiron. "Using Analytics to Improve Customer Engagement." In *The 2018 Data & Analytics Global Executive Study and Research Report by MIT Sloan Management Review*, 30 January 2018 (https://sloanreview.mit.edu/projects/using-analytics-to-improve-customer-engagement/).

[3]Phelps, Nick, and Sophia Christakis. *The Current State of Marketing Measurement and Optimization.* Forrester Consulting, September 2018 (https://cdn2.hubspot.net/hubfs/1878504/Marketing-Evolution-Forrester-The-Current-State-Of-Marketing_Measurement-And-Optimization.pdf).

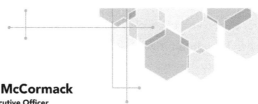

Leigh McCormack
Chief Executive Officer
Base Camp Health

The Subtle Art of Data Science

Surrounded by the hype of artificial intelligence, cloud computing, big data, and the like, organizations are flooded with prospective, data-driven solutions and techniques to solve their most complex problems. The vast offerings involving data science and digital technologies are quite the shiny, hefty hammers to have in the toolbox, but those tools need steady hands to guide them. That's where it becomes crucial to have deep passion, a solid foundation, and an understanding of context.

Context is the circumstances that form the setting for an event, statement, or idea so it can be fully understood. Context plays a part in every stage of the analytic process, from determining whether a problem can be adequately solved with data to the decision being made from the analytic output. There are multiple types of context that should be addressed to provide optimal value in data science, all of which are valuable on their own but are heavily interdependent. There are key ways to focus on these concepts and avoid possible threats that can disrupt the incorporation of context.

Types of Context

Data Context
Every analyst has heard of the 80/20 rule in the data science process. You spend 80% of your time cleaning and prepping data versus 20% actually exploring data and conducting analyses. However, what is often overlooked is that the amount of time devoted to preparation is usually exacerbated due to lack of context. Most data scientists will quickly resort to searching

for coding errors, sampling bias, or tuning parameters if outputs don't match their hypotheses. Rather, focusing more on how and why data is collected can ensure the proper evaluation of limitations on usage and interpretation downstream.

The collection, storage, and intentions of data do not exist in a vacuum. A data scientist's test in mastering data context is to be able to adequately adapt to limitations in the data, such as bias, censoring, and lack of representation. This adaptation can lead to improvements in feature engineering, dimensionality reduction, and analytical power.

Domain Context

While subject matter expertise develops with time and experience, this shouldn't be confused with domain context. Underlying knowledge of the policies, standards, and history of data generated in a given vertical impacts the outcomes and interpretation of analytics. A quick internet search should provide enough domain context to understand what has been attempted and what may impede success.

Methods Context

Methods in data science are ever-evolving, with new techniques, tools, and best practices emerging rapidly. However, the primary objective remains the same: to minimize error and noise so that generalizable inferences can be made. Understanding what drives variation in measurement, underlying characteristics, or time can lead to finding the most appropriate method faster and optimizing results.

Application Context

Perhaps all types of context culminate in the application of analytic output. It isn't uncommon for data science projects to stall or miss the mark because the output is not applicable. It could be because the output lacked interpretability or because the problem was poorly understood (perhaps due to a lack of domain context). George Box would agree that the value of analytics rests in its applicability. The true mastery of application context lies in being able to work the entire analytic process focused on how a single data point will impact both the user and future analytics.

Value of Context

There are two main value-adds from focusing on context in data science. The first: using context to make the most of a key partner. You are one half of most every data and analytics exercise. Your partner? A machine. And machines don't have context. A machine can only answer the questions it's given, leveraging what tools and information it has at its disposal. The human-in-the-loop must be able to ask the appropriate question and know when it's time to try again, overriding the passive approach of the machine. If the analyst doesn't provide the context, the machine is liable to answer the wrong question.

Second, context makes storytelling much easier and gives confidence to any analytic effort. Context through storytelling is what extracts true knowledge from data. Contextualization is crucial in transforming senseless data into real information that can be used as actionable insights that enable intelligent decision-making. Remember that analytic outcomes must appeal to the perception of the user or customer, even if this isn't always reality. They must compel. They must prove value. The best way to do this is through storytelling, and without context, your story will fall flat. The famous WIIFM acronym ("What's in it for me?") conveys the same message. To persuade and justify with data, you must put it in context for the end consumer.

Focusing on Context

- Start with the end in mind to increase adoption and confidence. Step outside the analytic minutiae and ask yourself some basic questions. Will your insight be relevant by the time it is consumed? Will the user be able to properly interpret output outside its statistical relevance? If the answers to these questions are no, then you haven't applied enough application and method context to your design.

- Partner with a champion to integrate practical domain expertise. One of the best ways to improve application context is to partner with a champion who will ultimately use your analytic solution and can alert you to possible pitfalls and considerations. This is a way to overcome large gaps in domain knowledge. Plus, everyone loves a good one-two, data scientist–plus–subject matter expert punch, even if it has two separate brains!

- Keep it simple. We all tend to gravitate to the brightest crayon in the box, sometimes to a fault. Often, this causes us to inadvertently blind ourselves to a more appropriate approach, which poses a risk of missing critical data preparation and analysis steps. To use proper methods context, reset your library to always start with the simplest approach and determine where it is lacking before selecting the next best option.

- Opt for more context over more data. Big data has offered much promise in the data science world. However, this could just be a meaningless strain on compute power if a frame of reference isn't considered. Before rushing out to throw more data at a problem, stop to evaluate the gaps in your existing data.

Conclusion

It may seem obvious that the more you focus on the relative landscape of a problem, the clearer the solution becomes. In the business world, cash is king, but in the analytics world, context is king. A mastery of context in analytics might be mistaken for passion, and a passion for anything leads to better outcomes.

Leigh McCormack is a thought leader in developing and applying analytical solutions to complex healthcare problems. She has a passion for driving equity in healthcare through strong data foundations. Her academic background is in mathematics and biostatistics, and she is pursuing her doctorate in health informatics. Leigh is currently serving as CEO of Base Camp Health, a healthcare technology startup focused on developing digital health solutions related to the proper identification and management of social vulnerabilities. She is skilled in guiding organizations in realizing the potential value in data assets and prioritizing analytic initiatives to achieve the highest value. In addition to her professional endeavors, Leigh is an advocate for the representation of women in the tech community. She serves on the board of the Chattanooga Technology Council and is an ambassador for Women in Analytics.

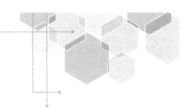

Jennifer Eigo
Instructor In-Residence
University of Connecticut

Beware of the Perfect Model

Many statisticians and data scientists are familiar with George Box's insightful quote: "All models are wrong, but some are useful." But what if your model appears to be not wrong at all, or only minimally wrong? Is it still useful? How can we figure this out?

Some of my university students found themselves in this very situation while working on their capstone project. They were tasked with building a URL classification model to categorize URLs into 12 possible categories, such as Business, News, Shopping, Sports, etc.

In a classification model, it is typical to have your target variable labeled with zeros and ones to indicate the classes, where "1" indicates the class of interest (the target class). In the training dataset, a URL like https://www.cnn.com would have a "1" for the News category and a "0" for all other categories. A URL like https://www.amazon.com would have a "0" for News, a "1" for Shopping, and a "0" for all other categories. The students built their training dataset according to those conventions.

When we were reviewing their model results, they hesitantly showed me results that looked really good — so good, in fact, that most of their models had a perfect Recall of 1. So why the hesitancy? Because any good data scientist knows that perfect models are nearly impossible to build.

The students had built a different model for each of the 12 URL categories. Table 1 shows the accuracy measures that they were reporting for each of the models. All the accuracy measures reported are very high, which at first glance might look like they built amazingly accurate models. But let's look at the Precision and Recall results a little more closely.

Classification Model	Total Accuracy	Precision	Recall
Adult	0.9254	0.9248	1
Arts	0.9403	0.9403	1
Business	0.9440	0.944	1
Computers	0.9104	0.9104	1
Health	0.8806	0.8801	1
News	0.9104	0.9104	1
Recreation	0.8918	0.8918	1
Reference	0.9328	0.9346	0.9959
Science	0.9627	0.9608	1
Shopping	0.9141	0.9141	1
Society	0.9515	0.9508	1
Sports	0.9291	0.9283	1

Table 1 — Initial model accuracy performance metrics reported by students.

Eleven out of the 12 models have perfect Recall. Recall reports how many actual instances of the target class a model can identify (see Figure 1). A Recall of 1 for the News category would indicate that the News model was able to correctly identify all News URLs without a single mistake! Great news, right?

Precision performance is also very high, in most cases greater than 0.9. Precision reports how often the prediction of the target class is correct (see Figure 1). For the News model, the Precision is 0.9104, which indicates that when the model predicts News, it is correct 91% of the time. Another solid performance metric!

Figure 1 — Calculations for Precision and Recall.

What Seems Too Good to Be True Usually Is

So why the concern? Firstly, a perfect Recall of 1 is very hard to achieve. Secondly, the URLs are spread out across 12 classes. Assuming the original data was balanced across all 12 categories, each individual model would be trying to identify a category that only occurs one-twelfth of the time. Let's say that there are 100 URLs for each category. News would be present only 100 times out of a total of 1,200 rows in the dataset. So that is not a very easy classification problem with such unbalanced data for each individual model. Thirdly, it is very unusual to have the Total Accuracy and Precision match exactly.

After some discussion with the students about their approach, I figured out what was going on. Their model performance appears so much higher than it actually was because they were reporting against the wrong class. For each model, they were trying to predict the "1," which means that a URL is in the category for the corresponding model. So for the News model, the target class is a "1," indicating News, while a "0" indicates that it is not News. However, they were calculating Precision and Recall assuming that "0" was the target class. This mistake in their Precision and Recall numbers was masking the fact that most of their models were actually predicting nothing but "0" the entire time!

Let's look at the math behind this mistake with some sample numbers. Imagine the training dataset had 1,200 records, and 100 of them were News URLs. If a model predicted only "0," the confusion matrix would look like the one in Figure 2. Here we can clearly see that the model is useless. It never predicts News, which is the target class and the thing of interest. Recall is equal to 0, and Precision can't be calculated because you can't divide by zero.

		Predicted	
		0	1
Actual	0	1100	0
	1	100	0

Precision = 0 / (0 + 0) = Error
Recall = 0 / (100 + 0) = 0

Figure 2 — Confusion matrix with Precision and Recall calculations for "1" as the target class.

Now let's instead assume that "0" is the target class and see how that changes the calculations. The model itself is unchanged. It is still predicting only "0" for every record in the dataset. The only thing that's different is the location of the zeros and ones in the confusion matrix to align with the convention of having the target class to the right and to the bottom as shown in Figure 3. Now when we calculate Precision and Recall relative to the "0" prediction, we get very different results. We get a perfect Recall and a very high Precision, which exactly matches the percent of non-News URLs in the dataset (1,100 out of 1,200, or 91.67%). This is exactly the mistake that the students made.

Predicted

		1	0
1		0	100
0		0	1100

Precision = 1100 / (100 + 1100) = 0.9167
Recall = 1100 / (0 + 1100) = 1

Figure 3 – Confusion matrix with Precision and Recall calculations for "0" as the target class.

How to Avoid Building Uselessly Perfect Models

So how did the students end up with a model that seemed nearly perfect yet was actually completely useless? They made a few novice mistakes that are easily preventable with a little extra care. Here are three things you can do to avoid building models that are similarly useless.

1. In case this isn't obvious by now, make sure you know your target class. The students' models were appearing so much better than they actually were because they weren't reporting important performance metrics relative to the correct class. Depending on the software you use, this can be a big problem. In some software or coding languages, if you don't specify the target class, the code will make an assumption. This assumption is often based on alphabetical order. In this case, "0" comes before "1," so it is assumed to be the target class. I've also seen this happen when the target variable is coded as "No" or "Yes." Because "No" comes first alphabetically, it is mistakenly reported as the target class.

2. Don't just rely on summary statistics when evaluating model performance. When discussing the model results with the students, the first thing I asked to see was their confusion matrix. After some hesitation on their part, it was clear to me that they hadn't even looked at it. While summary statistics are important, so many of them are calculated from

the confusion matrix that it shouldn't be overlooked. It is important to look at it to see what kinds of mistakes your model is making and in what quantities. If the students had looked at their confusion matrices, they would have immediately seen the problem that their models were only predicting "0."

3. Make sure you know what your code is doing. While it's easy to find modeling code on the internet to copy and run, it is crucial that you know the underlying theory behind it. Anyone with basic coding skills can throw data at a model. What sets the experts apart is the knowledge to apply the code intelligently and to correctly interpret the output. So how do you learn what the code is doing, especially in an open source world that doesn't always include documentation? Start with a dataset that you are very familiar with, something that you have worked with a lot and are already confident of the patterns and predictive power within it. Try out new code on that first. While there will be some variation based on algorithms, there shouldn't be any big surprises. And if there are, then it probably means that you need to better understand what the code is doing.

The students went on and fixed their target class, used oversampling to address the unbalanced data, and retrained their models, paying careful attention to their confusion matrices. This extra effort yielded much more realistic results than their previous seemingly perfect models. While their new models were certainly wrong, they were definitely more useful.

Jennifer Eigo is an instructor-in-residence at the University of Connecticut, where she teaches in the Masters of Business Analytics and Project Management program. Her focus on experiential learning is seen both in the classroom and beyond. In her role as associate director of UConn's Center for the Advancement of Business Analytics, Jennifer has extensive experience building relationships with external companies and guiding students through work on real-world analytics projects. Her prior professional experience includes work in business analytics and IT infrastructure in the insurance and utility industries.

Olga Berezovsky
Senior Data Analyst
VidIQ

User Segmentation and Power User Analysis in SQL

Scaling your user growth on your website or platform can be very challenging, and there are many strategies for doing so. One of these is to analyze user acquisition and measure user behavior by grouping your users into segments by the market or product definitions.

As a product owner, you should understand that only a percentage of your whole user base will return and buy your products or use your services again and again. Thus, the more you focus on expanding your user base and understanding user behavior, the more you can do to increase user growth and — as a result — revenue growth. To do this, a data analyst can help you sort your customers into the right groups, define a power user category, and provide a deeper understanding of your user base.

User Segmentation Technique

Quantitative user profiling is one approach to segmenting and defining user categories based on the data you collect. It helps to divide your user base into cohorts based on user activity level and your top marketing/product metrics: monthly/daily active users (MAU/DAU), user engagement, retention, etc.

Before we jump into analysis steps, let's clarify the definition of user profiling and a few terms first. Who are your power users? How do you define them? What actions do you look for?

Power Users Bring You the Most Value

As a data analyst working with different clients and companies, I run into various terms for power users — super users, influencers, whales, alpha users, etc. It doesn't matter what you call them, but it's important to understand which user actions you have to look for in order to define this powerful category.

The idea behind it is simple: your power users bring you the most value. How you define the value depends on your company size, sector, location, or product/service. Since we are speaking of user growth here, you have to aim for increased user acquisition. Therefore, the power users would share/promote your content and bring you the newest users. A common approach for defining the power user in marketing is to follow the process flow/funnel shown in Figure 1.

Figure 1 — Defining the power user in marketing.

- **Action:** a baseline user action event. The action can be a purchase, an order, signup, or even a simple "view event" if it fits your product model.
- **Share:** another user action, but dedicated to sharing your product or your content on social media or via other channels you offer.
- **Recruits:** users who are recruited by a Share action. Usually, these are new signups who come from the Share via a parent user. A parent user is often called a Recruiter, and the new clients they bring in are called Recruits.
- **Influence Score:** a defined complex metric that shows the proportion of recruited users for each Share action event.

Getting Power User Data in SQL

Regardless of how you collect and store data, you have to end up with a clean set of aggregated Action, Share, and Recruits events in order to calculate the Influence Score. Often data comes from various channels, like Salesforce or Google Analytics, and some of these events may already be stored in an RDBMS. Therefore, if the data is stored in different tables, you can create a temporary table or a view in a database for easier data acquisition. This will help you later with reporting. Below I will demonstrate querying the power user category using PostgreSQL and RedShift database (Amazon RedShift data warehouse).

Step 1: Get clean Action, Share, and Recruits data for the right period of time (I am using six months of data):

```
 3   recruits AS (
 4   SELECT recruiter_id AS user_id
 5          , item_name
 6          , COUNT(DISTINCT recruited_id) AS recruits
 7   FROM recruit_table
 8   WHERE created_at::DATE BETWEEN '2017-01-01'-180 AND '2017-01-08'
 9   GROUP BY 1, 2
10   )
11
12   , shares AS (
13   SELECT user_id
14          , item_name
15          , COUNT(DISTINCT created_at::DATE) AS days_shared
16          , COUNT(DISTINCT location) AS channels_shared
17   FROM share_table
18   WHERE created_at::DATE BETWEEN '2017-01-01'-180 AND '2017-01-08'
19   GROUP BY 1, 2
20   )
21
22   , action AS (
23   SELECT user_id
24          , created_at
25          , item_name
26   FROM action_table
27   WHERE created_at::DATE BETWEEN '2017-01-01'-180 AND '2017-01-08'
28   GROUP BY 1, 2, 3
29   )
```

As you can see, the first subquery returns Recruits data along with the recruiter ID. The second subquery gives Shares as well as share channels and share timeline, which I aggregate as days_shared. The third subquery simply fetches Action data for the same period of time. Make sure you query these three buckets for the same period of time.

Step 2: Assign an Influence Score and connect all subqueries together:

```
31   , influence AS (
32   SELECT user_id
33          , recruit_score
34          , share_score
35          , days_share_score
36          , channel_share_score
37          , NTILE(100) OVER
38              (
39              ORDER BY
40                    recruit_score DESC
41                  , share_score DESC
42                  , days_share_score DESC
43                  , channel_share_score DESC
44              )
45
46   FROM (
47       SELECT a.user_id
48          -- , COUNT(DISTINCT a.item_name) AS item
49          , SUM(c.recruits)*COUNT(DISTINCT c.item_name) AS recruit_score
50          , COUNT(DISTINCT b.item_name)*COUNT(DISTINCT c.item_name) AS share_score
51          , SUM(b.days_shared)/COUNT(DISTINCT b.item_name)*COUNT(DISTINCT c.item_name) AS days_share_score
52          , SUM(channels_shared)/COUNT(DISTINCT b.item_name)*COUNT(DISTINCT c.item_name)::FLOAT AS channel_share_score
53       FROM action a
54       LEFT JOIN shares b
55              ON a.user_id = b.user_id
56             AND a.item_name = b.item_name
57       LEFT JOIN recruits c
58              ON a.user_id = c.user_id
59             AND a.item_name = c.item_name
60       WHERE c.recruits > 0
61       GROUP BY 1
62       )
63   GROUP BY 1, 2, 3, 4, 5
64   ORDER BY 2 DESC, 3 DESC, 4 DESC, 5 DESC
65   )
66
67   SELECT a.ntile
68          , COUNT(DISTINCT a.user_id) AS users
69   FROM influence a
70   GROUP BY 1
71   ORDER BY 1;
```

First, I connect Action, Share, and Recruits subqueries and calculate a few interim metrics such as

- Recruit Score: Totals the number of Recruits for your product/feature
- Share Score: Returns the Share data for your product/feature
- Days Shared Score: Describes the sharing timeline
- Channel Shared Score: Displays popular sharing channels

After that, I assign the Influence Score for each user ID using the PostgreSQL window NTILE function, which is calculated based on the described scores below:

```
, NTILE(100) OVER
 (
  ORDER BY
   recruit_score DESC
   , share_score DESC
   , days_share_score DESC
   , channel_share_score DESC
 )
```

NTILE splits data into calculated groups and helps you rank the data from high to low. The highest score will be returned as 1 and the lowest as 100. Once again, you receive a proportion of users who have shared the most and recruited the newest users to the platform.

The final step is to fetch users who have the highest Influence Score (starting with 1). These will be your power users.

As the final step, you can filter this user category to include only specific returning users or to include only one product feature you want to explore or test.

Other User Segments Analysis

Using the same approach, you can locate other user categories besides power users. You can define passive or churning user categories as well and then compare them to find opportunities for bringing these customers back.

Another interesting user cohort to watch for is adjacent users, a concept developed by Bangaly Kaba, former head of growth at Instagram and Instacart. The adjacent user segment is a group of users who know about your product but haven't become engaged users yet.

According to Kaba, adjacent users "are aware of a product and have possibly tried using it, but are not able to successfully become an engaged user. This is typically because the current product positioning or experience has too many barriers to adoption for them."[1]

The adjacent user is critical to segment because it helps you capture the full potential of your product marketing positioning. To convert adjacent users into power users, you have to know who is successful today and why. This gives you a number of user features that help you to differentiate the "powerful" category from the adjacent.

Recognizing the adjacent users group is challenging. There are many personas for your product/service, but targeting the right user segment is very important. When it's done correctly, you will see the improvement in your user retention and engagement.

Conclusion

Quantitative user profile analysis is very common in product development, marketing, and advertising. It opens a lot of potential for crafting your product strategy. Segmenting your clients on power user and adjacent user groups, then analyzing their behavior and actions, is essential for scaling user growth.

Olga Berezovsky is a senior data analyst, data scientist, and big data enthusiast and evangelist. She has extensive experience in the big data industry — specifically in data acquisition, transformation, and analysis—and deep expertise in building quantitative and qualitative user profile analysis that reveals user insights and behavior.

Born in Ukraine and based in San Francisco, Olga is a writer for Data Analytics Journal (https://dataanalysis. substack.com/) and a member/volunteer at PyLadies, Women Who Code, and Women in Analytics.

Reference
[1]Kaba, Bangaly. "The Adjacent User Theory." *Andrew Chen* (blog), n.d.

Pam Castricone
Head of Data Science
InfoTrust

Using Analytics to Play in Everyone's Backyard

When I was in graduate school, my faculty advisor liked to say that when you have data analysis skills, "You get to play in everyone's backyard." What he meant by this was that analytical skills are highly transferable. You can choose the domain you want to work in: science, medicine, engineering, marketing, etc. I chose digital analytics because I could not imagine a more exciting, dynamic, and cutting-edge field to play in after graduation.

Before I was head of data science, I was a digital analytics consultant at InfoTrust. In that role, I was able to see how analytics is used across many different backyards, including e-commerce, consumer packaged goods, and news and media. We help our clients collect data about how their customers use their websites and apps and analyze it to provide better experiences. It is now easier and cheaper to collect and store data than ever before, and as a result, companies are amassing vast quantities of it. However, as the saying goes, quantity is no replacement for quality.

As a data scientist, I see my fellow practitioners enter the rapidly evolving field with various backgrounds and learn how to use sophisticated tools to uncover findings from the data. The availability of high-level programing languages and ample computing power has made data science an attainable career for many people, including myself. As the hype surrounding data science has grown over the past several years, so too has the number of tools making it easier and easier to apply advanced algorithms. At this point, I've read numerous articles describing how the future of data science will be fully automated and there will be little need for the data scientists themselves.

It's Complicated

In a recent project, my team and I were tasked with building a machine learning model to predict when a toddler is ready for potty training. Not having children myself, I lacked a fundamental understanding of the problem I was trying to solve — although I didn't realize that at the time. (I'm potty trained; that means I'm an expert, right?) The client provided us with several data sources, including web analytics, purchase behavior, and engagement with marketing campaigns. As analysts, we dove right in: we started cleaning the data, creating features, and getting ready for modeling. Our dataset had hundreds of features and millions of customers that we would use to uncover the hidden signals of potty training.

Except that's not what happened. Real-world data is often incomplete, inconsistent, and riddled with measurement error. Despite our thorough approach to extract every bit of information from the data sources, our models yielded underwhelming results. Each new model we tried produced only marginally better results than the initial logistic regression model, in spite of the increasing complexity. These sophisticated algorithms that can model the relationships within the data in complex, often opaque ways could not tell us what any parent could: it's complicated.

Our mindset for this project reflected a common sentiment in the data science community — namely, that with enough data, virtually anything is possible. It's easy, especially when playing in a new backyard, to rely on the data itself: "Surely, something in these hundreds of features must be predictive of my desired outcome." However, the increasingly sophisticated tools and techniques were no replacement for what was truly needed: subject matter expertise.

We learned that we needed to do our homework. We needed to immerse ourselves in the domain to understand which factors have a causal relationship with the outcome we were trying to predict. We read research articles; interviewed friends, family, and co-workers; and got feedback from the client's consumer research team. We realized that we needed to make a subtle but important revision to our problem statement: what we're truly modeling is when the parent is ready to start potty training their child, not when the child is ready.

We ultimately identified 13 different factors that impact a parent's decision about when to start potty training, and only five of them could be inferred from the data. The others indicated that, like many parenting decisions, potty training is deeply personal. Among other things, it depends on cultural values, socioeconomic status, time of year, the number of caregivers in the home and whether they work full-time, and the child's interest in learning. If a parent is putting off potty training until they can take a few days off from work (as my mother did), their purchase history and web analytics data will provide no indication of that.

Moving Into a New Backyard

I'm sharing this story to emphasize the importance of domain knowledge alongside the technical expertise needed for predictive modeling. Data scientists often talk about GIGO (garbage in, garbage out) when it comes to data collection and cleaning (i.e., poor-quality data invariably produces a poor model). Less is said about questioning the relevance of the data that is proposed to solve a particular problem. Vast quantities of data are collected because it's easy and affordable to do so, often without a plan for how it will be used. I've seen many data collection decisions made with a "Let's just collect it and we'll figure out what to do with it later" rationale. Then when an important business question is raised, it's assumed that the data we have must hold the answers. With our potty-training model, we learned that sometimes it doesn't.

Our findings led us in a different direction than we originally anticipated. Without data on many of the most important factors that impact potty training, the precisely targeted marketing audiences that we typically build were not possible. As next steps, we're evaluating bringing in additional data sources based on our understanding of the causal factors and the level of effort. And even though I've taken a critical view as I've reflected on the project, the audiences produced by our models were valuable because they provided substantial improvement over the CRM-based audiences that the client was using previously.

As analysts and data scientists, we have many opportunities to apply our skills to new domains, and I'm grateful that I've been involved in a diverse set of projects over the years. When you find yourself moving into a new backyard, though, instead of just playing, I'd encourage you to be humble, curious, and — most importantly — willing to pitch a tent and stay a while.

Pam Castricone is head of data science at InfoTrust, where she helps e-commerce retailers and CPG organizations uncover greater insights and value from their data assets. Specializing in statistical and machine learning models, she applies these advanced analytical techniques to drive better ROI than traditional methods. As a Google Cloud Certified Professional Data Engineer, Pam also helps her clients put their models into production in the cloud to drive long-term usability and success.

Pam is an adjunct professor at the University of Cincinnati's Lindner College of Business, where she teaches a graduate-level course on digital analytics. When she isn't analyzing data, Pam enjoys reading, the arts, and going out for brunch.

Ritika Gunnar
VP, Data and AI Expert Labs
IBM

Creating a Culture AI Can Thrive In

AI is completely reinventing the way we work, in all industries. It's poised to drive immense value across organizations seeking solutions that will enable them to get the maximum value out of their employees, their workflows, and all the data they're collecting. These are exactly the benefits AI can provide — AI can streamline processes, augment employees' skills, save on costs, and keep customers happy.

Today's unique set of crises and challenges has accelerated the adoption of AI across all industries as digital and data become increasingly critical. AI's ability to rapidly scale and provide useful information during the Covid-19 pandemic has given many people a glimpse into ways that AI can be a safe, easy-to-work-with solution. So the question we should be asking is: why isn't everyone using it?

AI Is Not a Push-Button Solution

More than any other technology that's been introduced in recent years, AI demands you make changes throughout your organization in order to see the maximum benefit. It takes a balance of components to end in a successful application of AI.

Some steps are obvious, like having clearly defined and easily measured goals at the outset, ensuring the technology you're using is up-to-date, and building a strong cross-functional team to shepherd the technology into your organization. What's less obvious is that your team needs to have a core ethos that drives them to embrace changes and to problem-solve in the face of setbacks. By creating a culture of curiosity, you are creating an atmosphere where imminent failure means questions are asked and solutions are tried until answers are found. Perhaps most importantly, that culture of curiosity must be one that is demanded from the top. You must be willing to instigate change or be the change agent in your company to facilitate the mindset that breeds successful AI.

Curiosity Is a Winning Attitude

I recently had the opportunity to speak with Michael Meyer, the chief risk and innovation officer of MRS BPO, a large call center company that processes about US$8 billion in transactions across more than 20 million unique customers. Michael had a vision to create an AI presence that wrapped around his entire business, enabling not only fast, effective communication, but also enshrining consistency and compliance throughout the company.

Michael understood that curiosity was key and tried for a full year to realize his vision. After a year of challenges and setbacks, he finally stumbled upon IBM Watson and was able to find success. It was his vision and curiosity that kept him pushing his team to look beyond consumer-level chatbots or custom-built but difficult-to-scale solutions. They eventually found a solution that worked for them and built Adam, a conversational AI that has reduced customer wait times by 100% and allowed MRS's human agents to interact with customers that need human empathy and problem-solving.

A perfect illustration of how a culture of curiosity solves problems comes from MRS as well. Michael's team realized early on that their chatbot didn't sound like a person; it sounded more like the technologists who were tasked with building it, making customer service less personal and ultimately less effective. Knowing a public-facing chatbot needs to reflect the way customers use natural language, Michael hired liberal arts majors to teach the virtual assistant how to sound like a person.

To find success, you need a cross-functional team guided by data and curiosity. Success with AI requires enabling creative solutions because, while it may sound trite, with AI you get what you put in. Rigidity will not get you flexibility.

Curiosity Stimulates Innovation

Getting exactly what you need from your AI solution is governed by the quality of your data. No amount of AI can overcome lack of data or low-quality data. If your AI is learning based on flawed data and narrow models, it will come to false conclusions.

Here's another point in your journey to AI where culture becomes extremely important. Building an effective AI solution demands many diverse voices. Without putting that basic building block in place, you may be setting your team up for failure. You need to keep open to the idea that different people, from different backgrounds, will have different approaches to problem-solving. These differences in thought are what stimulates innovation and business transformations.

I cannot stress how crucial it is to have access to new ideas when working with AI technology. With new ideas, you accelerate progress with both the technology and the outcome that the technology delivers. The culture of curiosity you've built will continue to extend to your consumer base as they interact with your technology.

Fostering a robust and curious culture enables a winning team and counters the average lifespan of skills in the technology market. The skills needed in the field of AI have a lifespan of about three to five years. Remaining static and traditional will cripple your outcomes and sometimes invalidate all the work you've done. We've found that many companies have had success bridging the gap between hard and soft skills using AI to bolster the entire workforce and not just a single employee or team.

In our work, we look for people who have varied backgrounds (not necessarily in technology), have been able to solve complex problems, and show that they have that hunger for continuous learning — that's the most important characteristic. And if you can augment that with emotional intelligence — really understanding not only the technology, but the people and the process pieces — you can go a long way.

Diversity Means Success

In life, the more diverse a team, the better the outcomes. The same thing is true for AI. Many people who are proficient in AI come from a philosophy or sociology background. So if you have the culture of curiosity in place, and can foster the ability to learn, you can blend in the technology aspects quite easily. Your customer support person becomes not just somebody who answers generic questions, but someone who can work on deep, complex issues. This means the profile of your support person must change to that of a person who is more knowledgeable. General questions and tasks can be answered immediately and effectively by conversational AI, but it still takes humans to solve human problems, and in general, human problems are as individual as the people experiencing them.

AI is a technology that demands diversity. We've all seen the embarrassing failures to come out of AI. Those failures come not from malice, but from narrow datasets and traditional thinking that doesn't confront its own bias. That's why it's critical not to just do AI, but to do it right.

The Formula

I started as a coder; now I lead a team of more than 1,200 highly technical experts, focused on advising, architecting, and delivering client success with data and AI.

Over years of observing how companies — through trial and error — infuse and scale AI solutions throughout their organizations, I've also seen firsthand the incredible benefits AI can quickly bring. My team's takeaway is the recipe for successful business outcomes: use the right technology, the right methodology, and the right skills and culture.

Ritika Gunnar is the vice president of Data and AI Expert Labs at IBM. In this role, she leads a team of highly technical consultants who accelerate clients' journeys to AI with consultative services, industry expertise, and architectural solutioning. Prior to this role, Ritika was the vice president of offerings for IBM Watson and many other parts of the data and AI portfolio. She is a data and AI enthusiast. Ritika joined IBM as a software engineer and has held numerous development and support roles in her career. She holds a BS in computer science and an MBA from the University of Texas at Austin. She currently resides in New York.

Alison Magyari
Manager, Business Analysis, Business Intelligence Center of Excellence
Eaton Corporation

Analytics + Design Thinking = Game Changer

Something needed to change. It was go-live day for my ninth large analytics initiative at Eaton, the power management company where I work. I was exhausted from the months of requirements gathering, visualization creation, daily meetings with the development team, and grueling testing cycles. I should have felt relieved that another project was going into the production environment, but instead I felt disappointed. I had the gnawing feeling that, where our dashboards and reports were going, they would be used sporadically, with users questioning the data and poking holes in the reports if they didn't indicate to them what they thought they should. I envisioned the entire effort ending up orphaned.

I kept thinking, "There's got to be a better way!" There has to be a way where we can work with our users in a more collaborative fashion, where we can show users different visualization options for their data before they're locked in to one way of seeing it for the life of the dashboard. There's got to be a way to enable our users to articulate to the team exactly what they're looking for — and what decision they're driving for — rather than just recreating the same 50-column spreadsheet that they will export from our new fancy toolset and manipulate offline.

I began to immerse myself in Google searches, hearing the same pain points across analytics projects from multiple angles. I went to roundtables with local companies where I heard stories about lack of adoption and frustrated users ping-ponging back and forth. I was thinking I was on a hopeless chase, until one day I read an article about design thinking. As soon as I finished the article, I could feel the lightbulb in my head turn on brightly. This is what we were missing! This is what could change our analytics projects from same-old, same-old to useful and engaging.

Design Thinking to the Rescue

Design thinking is a method for practical and creative problem-solving that is made up of three pieces: empathy, iteration, and invention. At its core, it involves understanding business users' needs and creatively discovering solutions to meet them. It is a process that allows you to dive in and determine who the real users of the solution will be and to deeply understand what they think, feel, see, hear, and do on a daily basis — and improve upon their frustration points.

It starts with the analytics team's ability to give a better future to its business partners. It also acknowledges that both the analytics team and the business users probably won't get the requirements right the first time. It closely aligns with Agile methodologies, allowing users to see iterations of work, requesting feedback, and allowing changes to the work before the final product is delivered. It has proven to be the missing link on analytics projects here at Eaton.

When we first started to roll out design thinking, I admit there was skepticism within IT. Not often do you hear the words "empathy" and "users' feelings" thrown around in the male-dominant IT field. However, seeing the low adoption rates of previous projects that had gone live, the team agreed that trying a new approach was worth a shot.

Empathy

We started with doing a stakeholder analysis. We wanted to understand who was actually going to be using the dashboards and reports at the time of go-live. In the past, we were often gathering requirements from an analyst who understood the questions that decision makers wanted help in answering. However, they generally didn't grasp the nuances of the data and which filtering options were needed in order to be nimble; plus, they wouldn't directly be using the solution once it was delivered.

162

When we discovered the users who actually would be using our product, we then switched to ethnographic research. We asked the users to show us how they do their jobs today. We watched them combining data from multiple disparate sources, creating pivot tables, and manually compiling data to get to the report they were being asked for. We made lists of potential points where errors could result from the cumbersome current-state processes and came back to them with ideas for how to automate data pulls and compilation. This could give the users time to actually analyze the data instead of simply working their way through the process.

Users would tell us, "I hate doing this!" or "I dread month-end because I have to do this process five times to get the output I need." Hearing those pain points, we knew what we needed to avoid in our future state. We educated ourselves on the best approaches to presenting data so that it would be visually appealing and easy to read, digest, and comprehend. If our users didn't understand one visualization, we simply showed them other ways it could be done until they felt comfortable with it.

Iteration and Invention

As our development team put our plans into action, we started meeting with our business partners a few times a week — if only for 15 minutes — to show them the development work that was completed in real time. If a change was needed or we discovered a misunderstanding, we were able to fix the issue quickly and show our users the next iteration in our next review instead of waiting until user acceptance testing.

Always we maintained open and honest communication, not blaming our users if they wanted a change and not beating up our developers if they created something that wasn't quite as expected. And at the end of the day, we created a better product. A more honest product. A product that could easily be consumed and whose value was evident because it was created based off of the users' real experience.

A Better Way — for Both Sides

Design thinking has changed our analytics team. It made us realize that there is a better way — a more user-centric way — to get the job done. We realized that if we continued to do things the same way we always had, business frustration would continue to mount, and eventually we would be irrelevant.

In a lot of ways, design thinking is just going back to the basics. What problem are we trying to solve? What issues do we have in solving it today? How can the analytics team make life easier for decision makers? We learn more and more each day. At times, it's two steps forward and one step back, but we are continuing to make progress and see results! If your team is struggling with user adoption and low usage rates, try out the design thinking methodology — it's an absolute game changer.

Alison Magyari is currently the manager, business analysis, of the Business Intelligence Center of Excellence at Eaton Corporation in Cleveland, Ohio. Alison has a strong passion for data and analytics and has been working in the analytics space since 2011. She completed a certificate in data analytics from Harvard University Online in 2019, has an MBA from Cleveland State University, and earned a BS in business administration and information systems from Lake Erie College. Alison is active in her community, serving on the board of directors for the Domestic Violence & Child Advocacy Center of Cleveland, as a volunteer with the Salvation Army and Mentor United Methodist Church, and as an ambassador for the American Cancer Society ResearcHERS organization. In her free time, Alison is a 500-hour registered yoga teacher and teaches classes at local metroparks and breweries around Cleveland.

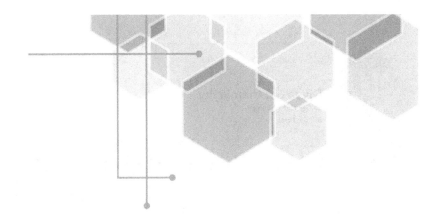

DATA VISUALIZATION AND BUSINESS INTELLIGENCE

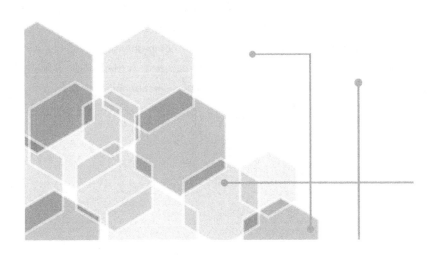

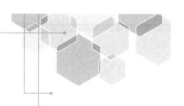

Divya Santhamurthy
Senior Data Analyst
REI Systems

What's on Your Dashboard: Data or Insights?

A picture is worth a thousand words — but what if the painter does not portray the right picture? Would you be able to grasp those thousand words?

This applies to data visualization as well. During the early years of my career, I presented my analysis to my data team members and folks from the business. My fellow team members got my point and applauded me, whereas the question from the business partners was, "What does this mean to us?" This question helped me realize that what I see through my numbers may not mean the same to my audience. It is not the numbers but the story behind the numbers that helps business people with their data-driven decision-making process. Ever since, my approach to analyzing and visualizing data has changed.

Once you analyze the data, the next phase — taking those numbers and showing the insights using the right tool — is both an art and a science. The goal is to generate an outcome that is simple, comprehensible, credible, and meaningful to the end users. The focus of this essay is to highlight five key areas that aid in building visualizations to unveil actionable insights.

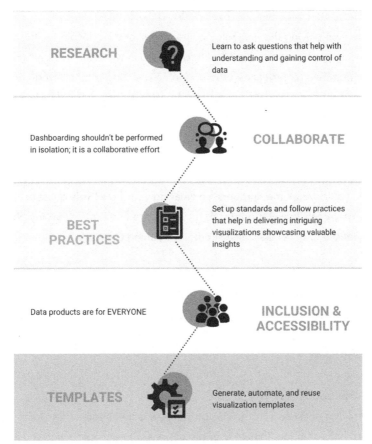

RESEARCH — Learn to ask questions that help with understanding and gaining control of data

Dashboarding shouldn't be performed in isolation; it is a collaborative effort — COLLABORATE

BEST PRACTICES — Set up standards and follow practices that help in delivering intriguing visualizations showcasing valuable insights

Data products are for EVERYONE — INCLUSION & ACCESSIBILITY

TEMPLATES — Generate, automate, and reuse visualization templates

Figure 1 — Key areas.

1. Research

The first task of a visualization developer is to conduct the research that helps with understanding and gaining control of the data they would work with. Start by asking the following questions.

Who Is My Audience?

Unless you understand your audience, you cannot deliver a product that is meaningful to them. Get to know their background, field of expertise, technical skills, and whether they are data-literate. All these factors will help you showcase the findings from your data analysis in the form of data stories.

What Data Do I Have, and What Else Do I Need?

If you are playing the dual role of data analyst and viz developer, this will be an easy question to answer. If not, get in touch with the individuals behind the numbers to understand them, double-checking with user requirements to see whether the dataset you have been given has all the data points you need. If there are gaps, research the missing data elements and talk to the analysts about how to acquire them.

What Do I Want to Show?

OK, you have all the numbers, so what do you show? This question should be user-centric and thought about along the lines of, "What insights are beneficial to my users?" Invest time in planning the story.

How Do I Want to Show It?

This pertains to the representation of data. What types of charts do you need to paint the story? It links back to your audience's level of comfort. Are they trained to interpret advanced visualizations, or should you look for simpler alternatives?

2. Collaboration

Involving end users in the design process is a vital piece for delivering a successful solution. Initiate user discussions with engaging workshops. The goal is to learn about the end users, gauge their understanding of the data, and assess their data needs. Create a mock-up dashboard based on your initial understanding and, if possible, develop this using the same tool in which you will deliver the end product. Show the mock-up dashboard to the users; ask them whether it serves their day-to-day data needs and what else would make it more efficient.

If you identify gaps in your interpretation of the business or the data, talk to individuals who can assist in deepening your understanding. After you create a design layout, team up with user experience (UX) experts and factor in their advice as well.

Another great way to refine your visualization is by conducting peer reviews. Gather your team, show them the product, give them some minimal background about the end users and their requirements, and ask them for feedback. Basically, you are trying to see whether someone without a lot of knowledge of the requirements can interpret the dashboard with ease and understand what you are trying to convey.

3. Visualization Best Practices

On average, it only takes an individual five seconds to judge whether they like what they see and want to explore a visualization further. So how do you create an intriguing, insightful dashboard that satisfies the goal of being simple, comprehensible, credible, and meaningful?

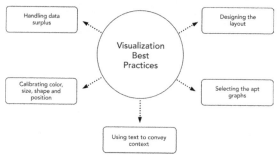

Figure 2 — Best practices.

Designing the Layout

Organize the dashboard based on logical questions the users would ask as they navigate through it. The first step is to place the most important insights at the top of the dashboard page. This should be followed by supporting information in the latter half. Do not crowd the dashboard; keep it to a maximum of six to eight charts per page. Create device-friendly designs by factoring in the devices on which end users will likely view the dashboard.

Selecting Appropriate Charts

Once you set up the layout, what comes next is choosing the right charts. This is not about what the tool offers or what you can create using the tool. The key here is to think about the visualization from the user's standpoint. For example, what is the point of visualizing data using a box plot if the end user does not know how to read it?

Using Text to Convey Context

Do not make the dashboard all about numbers. Use textual descriptions and include adequate context. Instead of showing a number, show what it means. To illustrate, see the difference in messaging between the two blocks below.

Figure 3 — Best practices: use text.

The former shows there were 78 new customers in the second quarter of a certain year. The latter provides context to say 78 is actually a 15% reduction in the number of new customers compared to the first quarter. This helps the business look into why the decrease occurred and take the necessary next steps.

Calibrating Color, Size, Shape, and Position

Invest time in understanding the science behind how the human visual system works to interpret color, size, shape, and position. This knowledge will assist in generating effective and compelling data stories. It is super important to label your visualization, provide color legends, and enable interactivity through filters. Once you establish these elements, it is critical to keep them consistent across the dashboard and its successive pages. For instance, you cannot show an "incomplete" status in yellow and "completed" in green on one chart and then change their colors to red and blue on the next. That leads to confusion.

Handling Surplus Data

What if you want to create a simple dashboard but you have too many data points — all of which, when put together, would weave a beautiful story? Consider revealing information as the user navigates through the dashboard. Include data points and graphs on the tooltips. Provide links to detailed information rather than squeezing it onto the main page. Another approach is to create role-based dashboards that show or hide information based on who is viewing it. Keep in mind that highlighting what is most important will help even a data-heavy dashboard capture the user's attention on the most vital data points.

4. Ensuring Inclusion and Accessibility

Data is the currency of the present era, and this asset should be accessible to everyone. Understanding your end users and conducting demos to determine how the dashboard is interpreted by people from different backgrounds are critical. Equally critical is the need to ensure that the dashboard supports interactions by end users who are differently abled. Nowadays, data tools come with inbuilt features that support these needs. For example, you can start by focusing on generating products that are color blind–favorable and screen reader–friendly.

5. Creating Templates

Consider setting up templates that incorporate standards and best practices. Most visualization tools provide means to create templates where you can program pieces like colors, fonts, sizes, alignment, etc. Design a template that best suits your organization. Automating and reusing this template will save you time that you can invest elsewhere, like the critical pieces of insight generation and data validation. The idea here is not to promote a one-size-fits-all template, but to establish a starting point that can be modified based on the needs of the end users.

A dashboard is worth a million data points, but the stories we convey using these data points is up to us, the ones who develop them. So let us ensure we develop the right stories.

Divya Santhamurthy is a data enthusiast who works as a senior data analyst at REI Systems. She analyzes data and designs and builds dashboards to uncover unique actionable insights. She is a certified Tableau Developer, and her data visualization works have been presented at national conferences in the United States. Divya takes pride in sharing her experiences and mentoring her team. She holds an MS in computer science from the University of Houston. Divya is passionate about empowering women and increasing gender diversity in analytics. She volunteers as technical curriculum developer for girls + data, developing and teaching learning modules to increase data literacy and provide middle school girls with hands-on learning in data analytics.

J. Michelle Maraj
Financial Systems Analyst
Lyft

Training Teams on Data Visualization

Data visualization is both an art and a science, blending diverse skills to draft a story out of rows and columns. Combining engineering, statistics, and design, the data visualization is typically seen as the end product, such as a summary graph or interactive dashboard. Training a team to create better visualizations can be tackled using a variety of approaches. In one training session, we can teach our teams best practices, such as what chart type to use or how best to use labels. But to achieve the most improvement in this field, there are many topics that need to be covered to boost analysts' data communication skills.

At companies where I have worked, I have had the opportunity to internally train teams on topics surrounding data visualization. There are many components to creating a data visualization: data, statistics, tools, design, and storytelling. A dedicated training week, or sessions over the course of a quarter, can help teams learn how to design a visualization from start to finish. It helps tremendously to have a handle on all five of these areas, but it can be difficult to teach on all of these topics in a one-hour lunch-and-learn. In a condensed time frame, focusing on just one area can still be beneficial for strengthening your team. So within each of these areas, what skills are important to learn?

Data

To even create a data visualization, analysts will need to access their data and transform it into the format needed for the desired graph. Some companies may have access to data resources, such as an engineering team to source the data, but experience in data will help analysts have conversations surrounding getting the information that they need.

The analysts may not be interested in learning how to set up a relational database, but it is still helpful to be able to read an entity-relationship diagram and to understand the different types of joins or data types. Rather than teaching SQL from scratch, some audiences may learn better if you give them starter queries regarding information they are familiar with and ask them to modify the queries to meet their needs. Analysts should also become familiar with how to handle uncertainty in the data and assess data quality.

Skills to teach include database fundamentals, querying (SQL), and analysis tips.

Statistics

Data visualizations are summaries of the rows and columns from your spreadsheet. A statistics background is crucial to understand what types of measurements best represent the data, whether that's deciding between using the mean or the median or determining whether the data follows a logistical or exponential curve. If it makes sense to draw a line of best fit or add a hypothesized forecast, knowledge in statistics helps analysts select the most accurate values to use.

When teaching statistics to a group of analysts, it is easy to lose their interest due to the mathematics background required. For a less technical group, it is best to teach by showing examples of how different techniques applied to the same data may produce dramatically different results. Aggregations are a great starting point — discussing whether an average is sufficient or a weighted average by population type would produce more accurate representations of the data.

Skills to teach include aggregations, regressions, and confidence intervals.

Tools

One of the biggest roadblocks to creating a data visualization is the tools themselves. Analysts may have access to Excel's chart templates or Tableau's drag-and-drop functionality but not know how to use them properly. Or an analyst may need to know how to program in R but have expertise in another area. There is always room for analysts to better understand the tools available to them.

Training on tools may involve demonstrating how to get data into the tool or how to write effective calculations to do the transformations needed. Depending on the company's tools of choice, it may be helpful to teach configuration tips or tool shortcuts. Knowing what is possible and seeing examples of creative ideas can be inspiration for future projects.

Training analysts to use a tool should be a hands-on activity. If the training session is short, encourage analysts to download the tool and data in advance so they won't need to spend time getting set up.

Skills to teach include Excel, R, and your company's data vizualization tool of choice.

Design

It takes a lot of work to get the data, understand the statistics, and learn how to use the tools. Many analysts get this far and then need guidance on the design aspect. Knowing what chart type to use depending on the data is crucial to ensure a visual is accurate. Understanding how to format the chart correctly is going to turn a visualization from a component the reader scrolls past to something a reader takes a few moments to better understand. This formatting may include labeling, colors, shapes, or even annotations.

Again, presenting examples of high-quality visualizations can help analysts understand why design decisions were made. Teaching design may involve expanding on a tool's formatting options or learning more about the company's branding. Rather than asking analysts to make a data visualization from scratch, a fun exercise may be asking for a makeover of an uninspiring chart.

Skills to teach include chart decisioning, color theory, and graphic design.

Storytelling

How effective is a visualization without a logical story? I can paste a bar chart below this paragraph, and it may be beautifully designed, but what value does it add to my essay? It is important to understand when and how data visualization should be used to tell a story. Especially in cases where a dashboard is developed, moving from one chart to the next should make logical sense. Analysts need to know how to make the graphs enhance one another, rather than giving the audience a data dump and making them figure it out on their own.

When creating a graph, it is important to add enough context so that the viewer can understand the story. To practice, analysts may be asked to draft a story based on a presented chart or to design a chart knowing the given direction a presentation should lean. Fundamentally, analysts need to under-stand how the data should be used and what conclusions can appropriately be drawn from it.

Skills to teach include storyboarding and written communication.

Training, Broad or Focused

I have had opportunities to teach data visualization over a week at a corporate retreat and over a quarter with weekly webinars, and in these multi-session situations, we have the opportunity to cover the full range of areas. Other times, the topic that we focus on may depend on the audience. If the audi-ence already knows how to create a bar chart but needs help enhancing it, we may focus on design. If the audience is experienced with reporting but needs help formatting data for analysis, we may focus on data.

Transforming your analysts into effective storytellers does not happen over-night. But with exploration into data, statistics, tools, design, and storytelling, your team will gain enhanced data communication skills with the power to sway audiences.

J. Michelle Maraj is currently a financial systems analyst at Lyft, where she is the lead Tableau developer on the Financial Planning & Analysis Systems team. Throughout her career, Michelle has been involved in training her co-workers in data visualization, with a goal of empowering them to be confident in their data analysis skills. A Certified Tableau Desktop Professional, Michelle competed as a Top 5 Finalist in the Women in Analytics Data Visualization competition and has had a Tableau visualization featured on Tableau's Viz of the Day.

Charlotte Weil
Data Scientist
The Natural Capital Project
Stanford University

Anna Häägg
Master's Student.
The Natural Capital Project
Stanford University

Interactive Data Viewers: Effective Tools for Spatial Planning and Decision Support

Decision makers informed with the most relevant knowledge of their landscape make better choices for future spatial planning, research shows. However, communicating complex scientific results — such as maps of ecosystem impacts and large, multidimensional datasets of tradeoffs — is an extraordinary challenge.

Today, we have an attention span of about eight seconds, and the abundance of information often feels overwhelming. To effectively convey scientific data for spatial decision-making, our research has found map-based data viewers to be particularly useful, especially when directly customized to the end users' needs and goals. In this discussion, we'll explain how such tools can effectively convey complex datasets to support informed decision-making and how to build them.

The Challenge of Communicating Multidimensional Spatial Data

Communicating multidimensional complex spatial data is difficult but crucial to support data-driven decision-making. This is work we know well at the Natural Capital Project, where we strive to develop science that addresses real-world problems and supports targeted investments in nature to improve the well-being of people and our planet. Based at Stanford University, our partnership gathers scientists from hydrologists to ecologists, but also economists, policy makers, and many more. We collaborate daily with governments, corporations, universities, and nonprofit organizations to equip them with tools and information to craft policies and investments that empower green growth.

Building on scientific rigor, we show where investments in conservation and restoration of ecosystems will give the highest return for people and nature.

Results of ecosystem services analysis consist of maps and tables, linking each point in space and in time to an ecosystem, and sometimes to economic values. For example, when analyzing water quality for a given region, decision makers might need to see the amount of sediments discharged into a stream or the erosion from each point on the landscape to make targeted management changes. Or they may need to know about pollutants leaks, the number of people downstream from a polluted area, or how vegetation contributes to retaining sediments and limiting erosion. Each ecosystem service leads to several interesting spatial results, and tradeoffs or synergies between ecosystem services can also be investigated, along with their changes over time under different future scenarios and development plans, adding a temporal dimension to each point of the map. These interlinked ecosystem assessments therefore output complex datasets that can be approached and communicated from many angles.

Communicating these complex results to decision makers and stakeholders in a user-friendly format is key to the success of a project. Clearly displaying the large datasets and highlighting the most important results allow decision makers to gain insights and make more informed choices. Poor communication of complex scientific results may result in confusion, misleading insights, or decision makers not feeling confident enough to actually use the results.

Using Interactive Viewers to Convey Complex Data

Viewers are web-based tools, customized to visually present metrics and key data through charts, text, and maps, which facilitate understanding of and access to datasets. In addition to being engaging and popular, interactive viewers are effective at conveying complex data. Interactive viewers have been found to facilitate discussions between different stakeholders as well as engaging a broader audience.

In the past few years, plenty of viewers have emerged and been widely used for spatial decision-making. Viewers have helped their users find illegal logging roads in South America (Global Forest Watch) and assess the damage to coral reefs after a ship accident (BIOMapper). From global viewers that visualize challenges like climate change, poverty, and air pollution (Resource Watch) to regional and local ones that display descriptive infographics with supporting data for offshore planning and environmental review (OceanReports), these viewers provide decision makers with the most recent scientific findings from all across the world.

Interactivity allows users to explore the data in the most intuitive way, with connected views of interlinked datasets, zoomable maps of high-resolution spatial layers, charts and legends directly linked to maps, etc. They enable scientists to visually connect people, locations, and data, thereby supporting data-driven decision-making.

Viewers also have the potential to reach audiences beyond readers of scientific literature. For example, one of our project-specific global viewers — which models nature's contribution to people globally — captivated over 20,000 users in the first six months after its launch. A number of these users found the viewer through social media, which is unusual for scientific communication. Another example is NASA's Gradient Fingerprint Mapping, which maps sea level rise based on changes in glaciers' ice thickness; it counts over 200,000 page views.

While these viewers are clearly engaging and exciting, it is worth noting that building such tools is significantly time-consuming. To assess whether such effort is worth it, we can measure viewers' impact. Using evaluation methodologies from the field of human-computer interaction and visualization, such as visual data analysis and reasoning, we evaluated dozens of viewers. We found that users gain complex, domain-relevant insights from data viewers, which confirms the tools' usefulness in supporting decisions. The research further showed that users could overview large sections of the data in only 10 minutes. Decision makers could also apply the insights they gained to create new hypotheses and potential adaptation plans.

Creating a Custom Viewer

For a viewer to be useful, design and implementation must be well thought out to ensure that the end users are not misled or confused. Figure 1 synthetizes design guidelines and principles for creating effective and engaging viewers. These were gathered from a review of over 50 scientific papers, in addition to a thorough analysis of 21 viewers and an in-depth user evaluation.

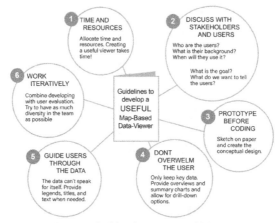

Figure 1 — Guidelines for creating a useful data viewer.

When creating a viewer, the main focus should always be on the end users:

- What is their background?
- Why should they use the tool?
- What is important for them to see?
- Are there any constraints, such as a limited internet connection?

Simply put, it is important to know the intended audience and the key message to be presented. Choices regarding descriptive texts, colors, and legends can then be based on the chosen user group. Moreover, designing visual representations comes with a great responsibility to accurately represent the data. Graphical integrity is important, and it is crucial to design the visual representations in a manner that truthfully presents the data.

Finally, testing the viewer with potential end users is critical to evaluating its performance. Interviews observing real-time usage of the tool are the most effective; however, surveys can also be used to get an overall understanding of the users' impression of the viewer.

There are commercial solutions for building viewers, such as ArcGIS Online, CARTO, or Mapbox. While these tools are great options for quickly creating something from scratch without any coding skills, they are often limited both in terms of data hosting and customizability. The alternative to using a commercial solution is to develop a viewer from scratch. This requires web development, design, and coding skills. While a variety of data visualization libraries exist (in particular, Leaflet for interactive maps and D3.js for interactive charts), this is still time-intensive work.

To facilitate the process of building custom viewers, we developed the viewerTemplate (viz.naturalcapitalproject.stanford.edu/viewerTemplate), a completely free and open source codebase that simplifies web visualization of spatial datasets (see Figure 2). It requires minimal setup and few to no coding skills. Anyone can customize it with their data to adapt it to their specific project. All underlying JavaScript logic is taken care of, as well the process for deploying the viewer online.

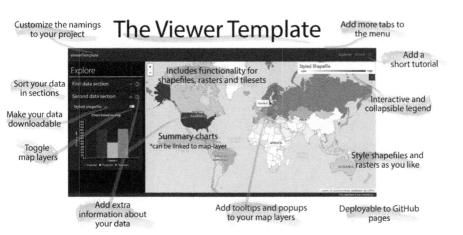

Figure 2 — The Viewer Template is an open source codebase for creating map-based viewers.

Conclusion

Interactive viewers are fantastically helpful in supporting decision-making. Effective, useful viewers are tailored to their audience and the key messages of the datasets. Design, implementation, choice of tools, and testing need to be carefully planned, preferably in cross-functional teams that include scientists, end users, and other stakeholders. When adapted to their audience, interactive map-based viewers are extremely powerful tools to support decision-makers in making informed choices.

Anna Häägg's background is in media technology and engineering, with a specialization in information visualization and human-computer interaction. At present, she is finalizing her MSc from Linköping University, Sweden. She conducted her master's thesis with the Natural Capital Project at Stanford University, where she created and evaluated map-based data viewers.

During her years of study, Anna has engaged in several student activities, including serving as president of the female student association at both her home university and at the Swiss Institute of Technology (École Polytechnique Fédérale) in Lausanne, Switzerland, during her exchange year abroad.

Charlotte Weil applies data science to better manage ecosystems, building data-driven tools to support scientific and sustainable decisions for Ecosystem Services and Conservation at Stanford University. Her works spans from a global scale (e.g., modeling the world's future food sufficiency or detecting dams from satellite imagery) to very local endeavors, such as co-creating development scenarios with local stakeholders in the Amazon. She is also passionate about visualizing complexity for decision support and pilots the interactive data visualization effort at the Natural Capital Project (http://viz.naturalcapitalproject.stanford.edu).

Charlotte's background is environmental engineering and circus aerial arts. She received her MSc with distinction of academic excellence from the Swiss Institute of Technology in Lausanne, Switzerland. Prior to the Natural Capital Project, she worked and volunteered in France, Switzerland, Benin, Cambodia, Tanzania, Thailand, Turkey, and Tunisia.

Dinushki De Livera
Business Analyst
Unifund CCR

The Beauty of Data Visualization

Our world today is one of constant technological advancement. A festival occurring in China could be experienced by someone in the U.S. — through the screen on their phone — in real time, supermarkets can predict a customer's personal lifestyle by the items in their cart, and somehow social media just happens to advertise a product that you were thinking about buying recently. All of this is possible because of big data collection.

On average, one person's smartphone uses approximately 2 gigabytes of data per month. This data is pulled from social media, photos, music, videos, and other applications. Multiply that by the vast number of people who use a smartphone today, and you get the collection of big data.

Big data is the combination of structured and unstructured data. Unstructured data may vary from characters that might not make any sense to numbers and patterns that are messy. So what do we do with all this data? Where does it go? And how do we make it useful?

Big data in the hands of an analyst is better data. When data is analyzed, we see patterns, structure, insights, and — most importantly — information that we can gather knowledge from. However, analyzed numbers in spreadsheets or tables have their limitations. Insights and trends are time-consuming to identify, important information may be missed, and visually it's not very interesting. How do we transform this data into its best form? How do we make it exciting and effective?

With data visualization.

Data visualization describes itself: it's the act of visualizing data. But it's also more than that. It's transforming data into useful, effective, and clear information with which an individual can identify important insights quickly and easily. This is easier said than done, however. A poorly prepared visualization can be ineffective and/or boring. The following sections will guide you in creating an effective data visualization.

Who

One of the most important aspects of creating a meaningful dashboard/visual is your audience. Who will be using or benefiting from this work? Knowing the answer to this question will help you determine what data you want to use, the insights you'll highlight, and the types of charts and graphs you'll create. If your visual is going to be seen by a particular person as often as every day, then getting an idea about their personality and preferences could make a huge difference in your end product.

Understanding the setting of your audience is also crucial. A professional business dashboard will look and read differently than a public-facing poster. Knowing your audience is going to play into all the other key aspects that will help you create a powerful visual, so it is worth spending the extra time initially to get to know whom you're building your end product for.

What

The second key aspect of a visual is the what. What content are you providing for your audience? If the content in your visual is not relevant to your audience members, then you have lost their attention instantly. Let's say you are asked to develop a business dashboard showing your company's revenue. If you know that your audience is the executive board, you'll start off by gathering high-level data points: net revenue, gross revenue, expenses, etc. Next, plan what insights to show. Given that your audience is high-level executives, you're going to want to show them findings that they would be interested in. These might include trends in revenue on a timeline, which months or seasons performed better than others, products that did exceptionally well, etc.

In contrast, if this revenue-focused dashboard were being created for an operations manager, then you'd switch your whole point of view. A manager will be interested in a more granular level of detail, such as revenue generated by individual employees on a daily timeline. They may want to see highlighted insights regarding each product they lead, which states and cities are generating the best results, etc.

Even before designing your visual, you should establish the link between the who and the what and carry it throughout your process. However, there is another piece of the puzzle that cannot be forgotten: the how.

How

How do we visualize effectively? In the previous example, we established that your audience was high-level executives. We also understood that people in such a position would most often be interested in an overall summary view instead of a very granular level of detail.

Given this knowledge of your audience and what you will be showing them, it is important to understand that someone at that level may not have the time to read into complex charts and graphs. They may simply want to see the numbers and trends. An operations manager, on the other hand, would probably wish to interact with the dashboard more, digging into further data and doing their own exploring. A visual for this individual may have intricate graphs that are more exploratory and interactive.

There are many ways to make a dashboard effective and meaningful. I will harp on three methods that I constantly use whenever I am creating most types of visuals.

1. BANS

BANS — or "big amplified numbers" — are a great way to turn someone's attention toward important information. In a business dashboard in particular, you can use these bold, attention-grabbing numbers to highlight very specific data that a user would want to see immediately. A couple of examples of

BANS in a revenue dashboard could be: this month's revenue, today's revenue, the percentage difference between today's and yesterday's revenue, etc. BANs can be very powerful when used effectively.

2. Layout

The layout of your visualization is crucial when it comes to keeping your reader/user interested and involved. You don't want to lose your user after the BANs. Organizing your charts and graphs in a format that tells a story or follows a certain trail helps the user navigate through the visual.

When I create visualizations, I typically start off at the very top of my canvas with a title and subtitle (if needed) to introduce the topic. Next, I display the BANs, showing the most important numbers that my user needs to be aware of. The graphs come next.

The human eye most often reads from left to right (with the exception of some languages, of course). This has trained our minds to see a flow/trend going from left to right. Therefore starting with the most important chart at the top left, proceeding to the right with the next most important chart, and continuing on until your least important chart is at the bottom right is a great way to order flow. Then adding legends and filters in the top right corner, away from your titles, helps a user adjust the data according to their preferences. Figure 1 illustrates a simple layout of a business dashboard.

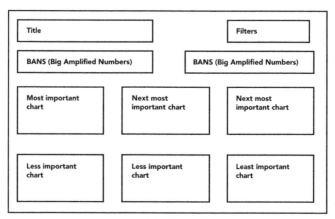

Figure 1 — Sample business dashboard layout.

3. Color

The use of color could make or break your visualization. Most people love to add color to beautify their work but may accidentally hinder that intention. A business dashboard filled with color can be distracting, misleading, and/or unnecessarily cluttered. In a grid of 100 squares, with 99 of them colored black and one colored red, which square is your eye drawn to? The red square. The difference in color stands out and draws your attention.

In a business setting, you could use this technique to highlight an important metric like revenue. If revenue is falling below target and you want to alert your user, you could use an alerting color such as red or orange. If it's safely in the target range, use blue. This way, even before reading the numbers or other details, your user is made aware of revenue performance by a simple change in color.

In a visualization, there are three common methods of using color: to categorize a variable, show a sequential trend/order, or display a diverging range. Imagine that you are attempting to highlight the diversity of products in a lineup, and you use a sequential range of blues to color the products. This detracts from your goal of displaying each product individually and instead suggests some sort of rank or order. In this case, you would want to use categorical colors instead so as to distinguish the products.

An obvious color pairing to show good versus bad or positive versus negative is red and green, but what if your user is color-blind? Those color choices would just be misleading. A good rule of thumb when choosing colors is to be aware of color deficiencies. If you're unsure whether the colors you are using could produce a color deficiency, cross-check with an online color deficiency test tool.

New techniques and trends are constantly evolving to improve the how, but the abovementioned features are simple but mighty when used accurately.

Conclusion

By incorporating the who, what, and how in visualizing big (or small) data, you have the power to grab the attention of your audience and tell them a well-organized story that can create awareness of a cause, persuade them of an idea, or provoke an action. That is the beauty of data visualization.

Dinushki De Livera, born and raised in Colombo, Sri Lanka, moved to Ohio to attend college at the University of Cincinnati, where she earned a BBA in economics and an MA in applied economics. Dinushki is currently a business analyst at Unifund and Recovery Decisions Science. In 2018, she won the Women in Analytics Data Visualization Contest with her "Women of the City" entry. In 2019 she was awarded Viz of the Year by The Tableau Wannabe Podcast at the 2019 Tableau Conference, and her Firebird visualization was shortlisted for the 2019 Kantar Information is Beautiful Awards

Leah Prince
Data Visualization Engineer
Humana

Business Intelligence: Data, Information, Knowledge, and Technologies

Technological advances have caused the digital world of data to explode. Organizations are surrounded by data that is structured, unstructured, and in various data types. Due to high data volumes, complexity of decision-making, the need to react quickly to changing environments, and competition among industries, business intelligence has helped many organizations perform deep dives to gain insights into their data.

Retailers, for example, adopt BI to learn more about customer behaviors in order to optimize marketing strategies. Hospitals use it to understand the flow of patients in order to ensure staffing is available at the appropriate times. Airlines are able to analyze airplane accidents to discover the cause and impact of the accidents and develop solutions to mitigate risk. Service centers use BI to understand service levels, determine training opportunities, and identify self-service solutions.

Business intelligence has helped many companies grow their revenue by using data to design marketing solutions. BI solutions have also helped many companies save billions of dollars by identifying risks that could potentially cause them to lose money. For example, some major distribution centers have incorporated BI solutions into their loss prevention strategies to understand the influences of loss for the company and how they could minimize those risks.

What Goes into a BI Solution?

Data, information, knowledge, and technologies help define the idea behind BI solutions. Data provides the building blocks to any BI solution. However, data does not provide value until it has been well prepared for analysis. Data preparation involves many steps, including identifying and handling missing values, outliers, discrepancies, skewness, and other anomalies in the data. Data with many flaws, such as these examples, will cause faulty decision-making. Therefore, it is imperative to ensure data is pre-processed prior to performing any analysis.

Once data has been pre-processed from its raw form, it can provide valuable information, such as the turnover rate of employees. The information gained from the turnover rate can be useful knowledge for making business decisions, such as determining a plan to retain employees based on the correlation of employee performance indicators. If there are any inaccuracies in the reported turnover rate and business leaders are not aware of this, they may spend additional funds hiring new employees who are not needed. Good-quality data is a key component of data integrity, which means having data that is reliable, accurate, and trustworthy. While some business people feel data can't be trusted, analytics professionals have the opportunity to change this opinion by prepping data thoroughly prior to analyzing it and sharing it with others.

The capabilities of business intelligence would not be useful without the technologies that allow data integration and connectivity, data pre-processing, and gainful knowledge. Many companies are turning to BI solutions to help get this needed value out of data. BI tools are just one component of a BI solution. These tools provide functionality that is able to connect to multiple data sources and extract, transform, and load data into data models for analysis. Also, most BI tools provide a visualization layer, which allows data to be presented in graphical form to aid in communicating results.

Sharing What You've Learned

Data visualization is like the pot of gold at the end of a rainbow. Data connectivity and pre-processing are surely important steps, but the knowledge gained is the ultimate goal compared to all of the preparation. The best way to present knowledge findings to the business is by visualizing the data. Similar to pictures in a book, graphs and charts are used as visual aids to help communicate the story by displaying patterns, trends, and correlations in data.

There are many different visualization options available, ranging from bar charts to pie charts, donut charts, box plots, line graphs, histograms, and geospatial maps. Each chart type has its own best practices, but it is important to note that each chart should be aligned with the appropriate data type.

Color and visual cues are known to help engage audiences, which makes them want to know more about the images they are seeing. However, the use of color should likewise follow best practices, as color can be a distraction if not used properly. Colors should be subtle; only use bright colors such as red and orange to call attention to items that should stand out. The true value of a visualization lies not in how pretty it looks, but in whether the information is accurate, the visual aids help tell the story, and the audience is able to interpret the message being presented.

Strategy Is Vital

Business intelligence offers many benefits. However, to ensure a successful BI solution, a well-defined strategy must be put into place. This strategy should incorporate the characteristics that are most valuable to the organization, such as infrastructure, scalability, user friendliness, ability to connect to current systems, intelligence capabilities, adaptability to the current data situation, and — most importantly — alignment with the business strategy. It is also important to ensure that a BI solution can function on many different platforms, such as mobile devices, if this is a characteristic that is important to the organization.

BI solutions require other actions to ensure they yield their hoped-for value. Involving stakeholders from the start to gain buy-in and support is vital to ensuring return on investment. BI tools can be costly, and an underutilized tool will not produce a good ROI. Therefore, stakeholders and potential users of the BI solution should be educated on the benefits of business intelligence and how to use the tools available to them. Having sponsorship and executive level support to promote these benefits will help ensure success.

Business intelligence has taken the spotlight in helping organizations answer some of the most important questions that are driving the outcomes we see today. In addition, technology will continue to advance and contribute to the increase in data volumes. Without a BI solution, organizations will have difficulty making sense of the data they have available and risk falling behind to industry competitors. BI solutions will allow companies to stay ahead by identifying and taking action on strengths and weaknesses in the overall performance of the company.

For over 10 years, Leah Prince has helped shape the way companies gain insights through data. Leah holds a master's degree in analytics and is currently a data visualization engineer at Humana. Prior to joining Humana, she served as HR quality support analyst at Lowe's, where she utilized BI solutions to provide information, knowledge, and recommendations regarding overall program health for the company's Human Resources Service Center. Leah has helped companies like Lowe's design and implement analytics centers of excellence, by designing reporting and analytics self-service options, as well as developing key performance indicators and dashboards for presenting information. She has also contributed to improving existing processes to make them more efficient and automated, reducing manual labor by 75%.

Leah is enthusiastic about discovering knowledge through data-driven approaches. Passionate about the contributions she has made over time, she will continue to strive to make a difference by using data analytics as her platform. She is an advocate for learning and reading about the latest technologies to uncover new remedies and best practices, to develop, and to grow. Toward that end, she has recently started a YouTube channel (https://youtube.com/channel/UCSOL9Xe15He8rZbHHpo2oTQ) to share her perspectives.

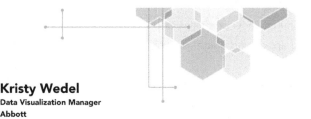

Kristy Wedel
Data Visualization Manager
Abbott

Choosing the Perfect Data Visualization

When answering a data question with visualization, it can be challenging to find the best way to display the information. Although there are general strategies on what may work best, it is crucial to keep the audience in mind when selecting one. The overall purpose of a visual is to convey insightful, actionable information. If a particular visualization doesn't hit home with an audience, it may not be the best choice even though it represents the data well. In some cases, simplifying or reformatting a visual is all that's needed; however, in other cases, it may be necessary to change the strategy altogether.

Asking the Right Question

The question the visualization will answer must be determined before selecting the appropriate chart. Visualizations that don't have one clear purpose generally fail to deliver. It can be tempting to create a visualization that will answer more than one question or a vague question, but the audience may not find insights in such a visual.

A first pass at determining the question might be something like, how are sales? This question can be improved by filling in more information about how we would know the relative status of sales. How are sales compared to last month or last year? Descriptive analytics deals with these types of status questions.

A next-level diagnostic analytics question encompasses why something occurred. Why are my sales up/down? Once you know whether sales are up or down, it's natural to dig into what is happening. Additionally, visualizations

193

might show predictive or prescriptive analytics that aim to predict what will happen and guide users on how to impact the outcome.

Determining the Best Visualization for Your Data

Once you have a solid question to answer, identify the type of data you will be dealing with. Is it discrete/categorical, such as gender or yes/no? Is it continuous, such as dates or sales? Different visualizations work better with different types of data. A line chart would not be an ideal choice to represent the number of men and women in a population, for example.

Some of the common types of visuals are:

- Bar chart — shows comparisons of categorical data
- Line chart — shows continuous data, values over time
- Pie chart — shows the percentage of the whole
- Scatter plot — shows paired numerical data
- Histogram — shows frequency of occurrences
- Box plot — shows distribution of data
- Waterfall chart — shows increase/decrease of intermediate values from an initial value

Bar charts, pie charts, and line charts are overwhelmingly used and work well in many everyday situations. Among data visualization gurus, though, the pie chart is generally discouraged. It is difficult to identify the spatial relationship among groups in a pie chart. It can be an acceptable solution when there are two groups; however, when there are three or more, it becomes more challenging to compare among them.

To find a better visual for the situation, identify the question's key elements. For example, to replace a pie chart that displays the percentage of male and female groups in a population, determine whether the goal is to see whether the groups are balanced or whether one is larger than the other. If the goal is to have a larger female percentage, a visual can highlight this and drop the assumed male population number. If the goal is to track the female population over time, a line chart could be a good alternative. If a snapshot of the female population is needed, a text KPI would be great.

Mix It Up, but Don't Get Too Exotic

Although bar charts and line charts can be ubiquitous and bland, more interesting visuals don't always achieve their intended purpose of conveying a particular message. Less commonly used visuals may confuse or overwhelm users and detract from their purpose.

Scatter plots are one type of visual that can benefit from additional instruction for less familiar users. Adding words or colors to a scatter plot can help draw the user's attention to the relevant information. Box plots can also benefit from clear legends and color to differentiate any other groups.

There are additional chart types that can break up the monotony of bar and line charts:

- Radar charts can be an excellent choice when you have multiple quantitative variables. These can become confusing when multiple groups are presented at the same time, however.
- A treemap is helpful for displaying a hierarchical view of data.
- Maps can show where something is present, and a layer can be added to display the magnitude of certain data points in a particular location. Although maps work well with most location data, it is essential to choose a map that fits the data well. If all of the data is in one small section of the map, it would be difficult to see much of a pattern if, say, a world map were used.
- Sparklines are useful in showing overall trends and highlighting maximums and minimums.
- Plain old tables, perhaps with some formatting, can be a fantastic way to display data. The pitfall of tables is that they often display auxiliary data that doesn't directly draw a user to outliers, trends, general insights, etc. Tables can be of great use for deep dives once a predesigned chart for that specific purpose (outliers, trends, other insights) has identified one of these as being of interest, though.

- Speaking of old-fashioned, words are another great way to present information to an audience. Many platforms allow you to combine preset text with calculated measures to display text. Text can help make sure a message is received without any potential visualization confusion. However, if the text is too wordy, it may be overlooked.

Finally, even though a visualization might generally be a good choice given the type of data and the question to answer, it may not be the best choice for a particular audience. If an audience is accustomed to viewing data in a specific way, changing chart types may make it harder for them to identify what they need. If, for example, they can glean value from a familiar pie chart, it can be best to present the data in the same format, while potentially also offering an additional secondary chart/KPI that will build upon it. The best chart for a situation depends on the audience, the question, and the data.

Kristy Wedel is the data visualization manager in the Market Insights Data and Analytics Team at Abbott. She graduated with a BS in mathematics from The Ohio State University and completed the data science specialization through Johns Hopkins University on Coursera. She has experience developing best practices; querying large, complex data sets; transforming data; developing predictive models in R; and creating dashboards using Qlik and Power BI.

Marian Fairman
Lead Analyst, Digital Insights + Integration
Progressive Insurance

How to Take Your Dashboards from Good to Great

The difference between good and great dashboards is straightforward: a good dashboard provides users with the information they need, whereas a great dashboard provides users with the information they need easily, answers additional questions they may have, and achieves both objectives with engaging design and a certain flair.

Many data analysts lament that their dashboards are good but not great. These individuals understand the technical part of how to make a dashboard, and they're usually experts on their data, but they're still not confident in their design ability to create a truly great dashboard.

In order to build great dashboards, you need to embrace three key practices:

1. Experiment
2. Experience
3. Iterate

Once you put these three practices into action, it will reinvigorate your dashboard skill set, and all your coworkers will be raving about how great your dashboards are.

*Note: This article is written focused on Tableau, but any visualization software could be used.

1. Experiment

In order to create great dashboards, you need to experiment. One of the easiest ways to do this is to participate in Makeover Mondays. Each week, two Tableau Zen Masters publish a dataset, and people all over the world create visualizations based on that data. Makeover Mondays allow dashboard designers to experiment on visualizations with an easy-to-use dataset. Since people worldwide are creating visualizations based on that same data, designers can compare their visualization against others and learn from that process. Even if you aren't a Tableau user, you can still use the Makeover Monday data with your visualization tool of choice.

I started doing Makeover Monday with my co-workers in 2018. Each week, we would download the dataset and create some kind of visualization in an hour. It might be great, it might be terrible, but at the end of the day, we would get together and review our creations. I primarily started this process to train an intern on Tableau, and while her skills developed greatly due to Makeover Mondays, mine did too — as did those of other experienced members of my team.

Now I conduct company-wide Makeover Monday sessions on a monthly basis. It's been gratifying to see other people come up with creative visualization experiments. For my experiments, I usually pick a new technique that I want to learn, which might be hex maps, Sankey charts, radial charts, or the use of unusual colors, backgrounds, or shapes. Since the experiment takes just an hour once a week, it's easy to set aside time to do it. Plus, it's fun, whether you're working by yourself or collaborating with a team. If you do Makeover Mondays regularly, you'll start to see real results as an outcome of your experimentation.

There are many other ways to experiment with your visualization tool of choice. You can join an online community of practice, participate in Tableau's Iron Viz competition or Workout Wednesdays, take part in the community-led Iron Quest, or build your own visualizations on interesting data. The key is to experiment in a way that pushes the boundaries of your skills. Because designing visualizations is as much a creative endeavor as it is a technical one (and in our workplaces, the creative side is frequently disregarded), experimentation is a necessary part of taking your dashboards from good to great.

2. Experience

In order to build a great visualization, you need to know what a great visualization looks like. All artists learn from the work of skilled artists, especially when developing their own style. You need to experience other visualizations and determine what is aesthetically appealing to you in order to develop your own technique.

The easiest way to do that is to subscribe to Tableau's Viz of the Day. Each day, Tableau will email you a visualization they consider great enough to share with the Tableau community. In two or three minutes a day, you'll expose yourself to lots of different ideas about what a great viz looks like.

Another way to experience great visualization is to browse the vizzes out on Tableau Public. You'll see the good, the great, and the ugly out there, but browsing the various vizzes will engender ideas on design. To experience great visualizations, you should attend Tableau's Iron Viz event. This is Tableau's visualization competition, which you could also participate in as an experiment. The feeder visualizations are available on Tableau Public, and the competition itself, which is watchable live or on YouTube, offers some great insights into different ways to create a viz.

There are also some helpful blogs you can follow — I highly recommend the Flerlage Twins (https://www.flerlagetwins.com/). Their blog posts are incredibly well thought out, and they offer a lot of easy-to-follow tutorials, including one for a Sankey chart that will knock the socks off your peers when you use it at work (I've done it!). You may also be interested in the chart ideas available at the Data Viz Project (https://datavizproject.com/). You can get some great ideas from there when your boss asks you to build "anything but another bar chart."

Staying current with training and participating in events like the Tableau Fringe Festival, a virtual conference, will also help you experience great visualizations. You won't like everything you see — and that's good. If there's a dashboard you like, try to download it and figure out how to duplicate it. Think of yourself like a painter, learning from the great masters, trying to figure out how to make a particular brush stroke, before striking out on your own with your own unique style.

3. Iterate

Experimenting and experiencing are the important first steps in getting your dashboards from good to great. The next step is to iterate. Basic charts are easy to create, and they provide a lot of information, but with some slight tweaks, or iterations, you can develop a visualization that more fully represents the story you're trying to tell.

Ditch the Default

The default charts and color palettes make it easy to create a standard chart. But you're not looking for a standard chart — you're looking for a great one! In order to get a sharper-looking chart, you can customize your tooltips, colors, fonts, borders, and gridlines to make your charts stand out. Experiment with different looks to find ones you like that are clean and easy to understand.

Use Custom Color Palettes

The easiest way to make a visualization look more professional is to forgo the default color palette. There's nothing wrong with the default color palette — it's the default for a reason — but using a custom color palette will set your visualizations apart from the crowd. If your company has a standard color palette, it helps to use that, and if your company doesn't, maybe you can create one using the logo and colors on your website. Check out the huge amount of color palettes on the color-hex website (https://www.color-hex. com/color-palettes/) to get some ideas, and then experiment with them on Makeover Mondays to find ones you like.

Professionalize

All dashboards should show the last date you updated the information and have a way to contact someone. A question mark icon that links to a contact email address helps your customers contact you.

Reduce Chart Junk, Increase Data Ink

This classic dashboard tenet tells you to remove everything that doesn't make the information more readily accessible. Try to remove gridlines, shading, axis lines, and headers to see whether your information is as clear or clearer with them gone. Always keep this principle in mind!

Don't Overdo It

You can fancy up the font and change your colors, but if you don't create a dashboard that serves the story you're trying to tell, it won't make it great. If you're using 10 different colors, no one will be able to discern one from the other. Try to remove all colors and use shades of gray in order to figure out what you truly need to highlight in color, then add color judiciously.

Get Feedback

To achieve a genuinely great dashboard, you need to get feedback from either your customers or your peers — or, ideally, both! Before you release a dashboard to your customers, find a peer who can help you evaluate whether your dashboard is telling your story. Find someone who's not scared to tell you when it's bad. For your customers, link your dashboard to a feedback page and then ask them for candid feedback. If your customers see you make changes based on their feedback, they'll keep giving you information about what they really need, which helps you deliver that great dashboard. Feedback is a gift (keep telling yourself that!).

Becoming a Standout

If you spend time experimenting, experiencing, and iterating, you'll notice that your dashboards will go from good to great. Your dashboards will stand out from the crowd and be celebrated for their attractive design. A little effort will go a long way toward making you a viz whiz.

Marian Fairman has been telling stories with data for 15 years. Currently she works at Progressive analyzing digital data. Prior to joining Progressive, she spent 10 years at Forest City Realty Trust in a variety of roles, ranging from analyzing commercial real estate to leading BI projects and managing a team of data analysts. Marian has evangelized about data and visualizations at Progressive, the Cleveland/Akron Alteryx User Group, the Tableau Fringe Festival, the Tableau Conference, and while guest lecturing at Case Western Reserve University. She has a BA and MBA from Case Western Reserve University. Outside of work, Marian is active telling stories with the Cleveland theater community and serves as vice president on the board of Dobama Theatre in Cleveland Heights, Ohio.

Gabriela Alessio
Data Scientist
Atlassian

Scandinavian Design Principles for Data Storytelling

Note: In this essay, "data storytelling" is defined as the collection of visualizations and supporting text used to translate qualitative or quantitative data into human-absorbable artifacts.

If you Google "Scandinavian design," the first results that you'll likely get are furniture ads and interior design articles. However, if you search for the definition of Scandinavian design, you'll find that it is actually a movement that flourished in the 1950s throughout five Nordic countries — Norway, Sweden, Finland, Denmark, and Iceland — based on the four principles of light, simplicity, functionality, and beauty.

While warm rooms full of light and white furniture might come to mind, evoking the recently popular *hygge* trend of promoting a sense of wellness through coziness, the actual ethos of this design movement is *lagom*, which means "just the right amount": not too little and not too much, just exactly what you need to properly function. Every element should be both pleasing to the eye and also serve a purpose.

Despite having architectural origins and historical applications to furniture (think: IKEA white foldable tables), "Scandi" design has transcended to broader industrial design, such as consumer electronics, cars, and mobile phones. Apple's iPhone hardware and software have both applied these design principles: clean, simple, highly functional, and visually appealing. Likewise, Tesla's Model S dashboard design team took away single-function artifacts and replaced them with one multi-function tablet. This is Scandi design in action: these teams performed addition through subtraction.

The Scandi footprint has also expanded to online user experience, yielding great insights into how to adopt *lagom* practices to provide clean flows that allow the user to focus on important tasks by hiding or deleting noncritical or low value–adding features that distract. Visual clutter can lead to mental clutter, so it is tucked away or not even allowed to build up in the first place.

The above demonstrates that the Scandinavian design principles are agnostic across physical and nonphysical spaces. The principles are great for not only maximizing interior spaces in a pleasing and functional way, but also capturing user focus — a key requirement for data visualization and storytelling!

Applying the four principles of Scandinavian design for data visualization and storytelling: It's not "less is more," it's *lagom*.

Data visualization and storytelling are just as important as the analytical and engineering work that happens before them. If you can't properly translate your findings into a cohesive narrative accompanied by visual evidence, all your work will have been for naught.

The "*lagom* compass" of Scandinavian design serves as a guide to harness the finite amount of user attention and maximize insight retention by ruthlessly questioning the amount of data, graphs, text, and even color hues that should be present in visualizations. Depending on your audience, the complexity of the analysis may vary, but not the need for focus on a discrete set of takeaways.

Light Content Design

Light in this context is not the opposite of "rich in content," but rather connotes a balance between the elements that are required for conveying the message. For ease of reading and processing, give similar visual weight to the insights, charts, text, and negative space you use in your visualizations.

A small number of insights can still have a mighty impact! On average, humans can retain up to seven things at a time and, based on their personal interest in them, store them for shorter or longer terms. Depending on the topic and complexity of your story, limiting the elements you use to the points you want to get across will help make the story lighter and shorter. Five or fewer insights are often ideal.

When it comes to content layout, there are three different types of balance in light design:

- Symmetrical: each side of the visual is the same as the other.
- Asymmetrical: both sides are different but still have a similar visual weight.
- Radial: elements are placed around a central object that acts as an anchor.

Scandinavian design tells us to use light to highlight the important parts of a room; your visualizations can use the same principle to highlight takeaways.

Simplicity for Consumption
From access to readability, your platform or delivery method should be easy to find and use. Starting off with a frictionless provisioning of your work is an important step to avoid spending the user's "attention calories."

Language should also be simple to understand. Knowing your audience and the reception context helps you fine-tune the terms and technical level of your text-based messaging.

Format and color can be used as tools to minimize distractions. Standardizing fonts and callout formats establishes patterns that allow the user to quickly understand what and where they need to place most of their attention — namely, on the "disruptions" to those patterns. Capitalize on making a small number of things stand out and use everything else to provide context and allow deep impressions of the key takeaways.

Scandi design relies heavily on neutral colors, most notably bright whites with pops of color. The overall spaces tend to be monochromatic, with hues coming into play as accent pieces that provide focus points. If you have to make a resounding emphasis on a data point or insight, this is a great way to draw undivided attention to it.

Functionality

This is where the deepest application of *lagom* comes into play. Every single visual element and bit of text should have a clear purpose. In Scandinavia, people are limited to generally expensive and smaller housing. In a similar way, the physical real estate and user mental space you have available are limited, so embrace the Scandi design principle that less is truly more and that every item really must earn its keep.

Don't be afraid to delete charts or move them to appendix sections if they can be useful for users who want to go deeper into detail.

Language and wording should always carry out two functions:

1. Communicating the facts
2. Communicating the insights from the facts

You can achieve these functions by indicating how the user should feel about the fact (e.g., up = good, down = bad) and why it's relevant (e.g., why is x being up good?). This helps denote the benchmark, the change against it, and the magnitude of the change.

Note: appendices should not be used as catchalls, either! Make sure insights in an appendix enhance your analysis or report; don't simply use them a dumping ground for every analysis avenue you explored.

Beauty

A well-designed and thoughtfully curated data story can go much further if it is visually appealing and interesting to read. Think about the most interesting stories you have read from well-known newspapers or magazines: they are usually not very long and perhaps offer just one important insight (light content), they are easy to read (simple access), they contain few charts (functional discretion), and they are visually appealing!

Good data visualization and information design help the data story convey interesting ideas, bend minds, and enable the viewer to retain facts.

Lagom and Prosper

As a data person in charge of communicating insights, you should think of yourself also as a designer. You have command over how light, simple, functional, and beautiful you can make the content to achieve the ultimate goal of captivating the user's attention with your story.

Your "designer" tools may be R, Python, Tableau, even Figma! Luckily, all of them can be programmatically adapted to a certain point to follow the design principles proposed here for the format, leaving more time for you to do the curation of insights and key takeaways.

Gabriela is a Mexican data scientist living in the Bay Area. She is obsessed with understanding users through data to help teams ship meaningful and inclusive products. Gabriela is also invested in helping open source software be adapted and applied to basic needs services to drive costs down for underrepresented communities.

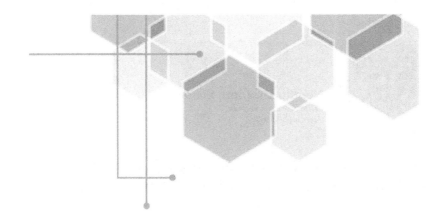

CASE STUDIES

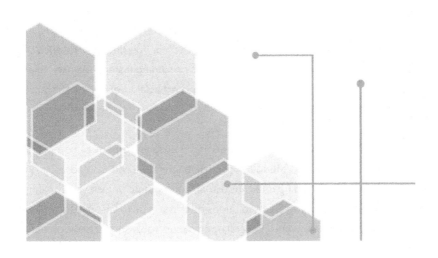

Neethu Elizabeth Simon
IOT/ML Software Engineer
Intel Corporation

Challenges in Implementing a Vision-Based AI/ML Solution for Textile Defect Detection

The Internet of Things is a web of numerous devices that are interconnected and interact with each other with minimal human intervention. Massive numbers of devices are getting connected, every second, to the internet and are collecting and sharing data. Gartner predicts that 25 billion connected things will be in use by 2021.[1] Thanks to cheaper and faster processors and wireless networks, more innovations in IoT are bringing the digital and physical worlds together. Since these devices are constantly communicating, collecting, and sharing data, smart systems can be built that can computationally analyze large sets of data to reveal patterns, trends, and associations.

As IoT comes to life, the number of things getting installed and connected is growing exponentially. Cameras are the ultimate "thing" sensor, generating an enormous amount of visual data. The ability to derive sense from this massive flow of data from cameras has become critical. With advances in deep learning, building a digital "visual cortex" for inferring the presence of specific objects in an image or video feed is becoming faster and easier than ever. Video along with computer vision and artificial intelligence/machine learning is now termed the "eye of IoT."

Fast and low-cost computing is enabling the development of computer vision–based IoT and AI/ML solutions, resulting in their widespread usage in several domains, including retail, industrial, autonomous vehicle, and healthcare sectors. Developing these solutions does not require vast programming expertise and complex tools. Several open source tools and technologies are available to build end-to-end high-performance computer vision applications that fuel AI from edge to cloud. However, implementing these solutions for real-world problems still poses several challenges, as the following case study will show.

Automating Defect Detection in the Textile Industry

During the fabric manufacturing process, defect detection is an important process for eliminating defective fabric pieces and maintaining high quality. Textile defects can be of different kinds, based on fabric texture and color. Currently, the majority of the inspection process is done manually by humans. Manual inspection enables the instant detection of defects, but due to fatigue, human error can occur and fine defects can go undetected. Thus, automated defect detection holds the potential to improve quality and reduce human labor cost. However, automating the defect detection process is not easy, as there are numerous textile defects defined by the textile industry[2]. Figure 1 illustrates some common textile defects.[3]

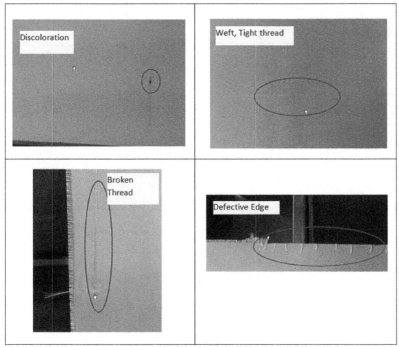

Figure 1 — Common textile defects.

211

Complex algorithms have been suggested in the past for textile defect detection, but practical implementation of these algorithms involves changing the inspection machine, which is expensive. Another option is to use computer vision and deep learning to train models and use them to detect textile defects in real time by modifying the current inspection system instead of replacing it.

With this goal in mind, my team — consisting of a hardware engineer, software engineer, and product marketing engineer — worked with a textile manufacturer, textile inspection machine manufacturer, and an original design manufacturer to develop a real-time, vision-based AI/ML defect detection solution for the textile manufacturing industry.

The solution involved integrating the inspection machine with cameras for data collection and a controller for real-time inferencing to detect textile defects (see Figure 2 and 3).

Textile Inspection Machine

Video Feed

Real Time Inferencing using High Compute Processor

STOP Machine when detecting defects

Figure 2 — Solution architecture.

Figure 3 — Implementation process.

1. Data Collection

This step involves acquiring and organizing data for consumption, including pre-processing to clean and remove any bad data. In this solution, data is collected as video and decomposed into individual frames/images. Training is done with both good fabric and defective pieces.

2. Data Annotation

This step is where the ground truth is established. Data is labeled to identify images either as good or as exhibiting one of two textile defects: discoloration and weft. In this solution, a binary and multi classification approach was adopted and images were manually distributed into appropriate folders for training (see Figures 4 and 5). Individual images were pre-processed and classified under the following directories (see Figure 6):

Binary Classification — 2 classes: good, defect
Multi Classification — 3 classes: good, discoloration, weft

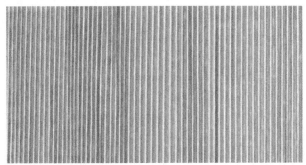

Figure 4 — Good data.

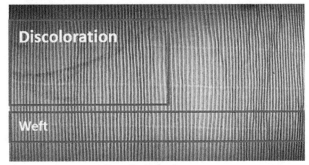

Figure 5 — Defect data.

213

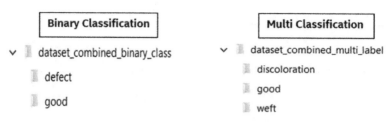

Figure 6 — Image labeling and classification.

3. Training

This step involves building the analytical model for classification. In the solution, Tensorflow was used for training, and the popular neural network classification model Mobilenet[4] was also used. Offline training was performed to develop the textile model.

4. Inference

Here the trained model is deployed to make predictions based on the new data that is received. For faster and secure processing, inference occurs at the edge computing device (controller), which does not require any connectivity to the cloud. Real-time inferencing and optimization were accomplished using the open source OpenVINO toolkit.[5] This toolkit is based on convolutional neural networks and extends workloads across Intel hardware (including accelerators) and maximizes performance.

Our models performed well for binary classification, producing an average 98% accuracy. However, multi classification accuracy was substandard. Images were pre-processed with the CLAHE (Contrast Limited AHE) technique to improve accuracy. Offline test accuracy was good; however, live inference testing results were unsatisfactory.

Where Challenges Arose

Hardware

Camera, Lens, Lighting Selection

- Accuracy of the trained model is heavily dependent on the quality of data used for training. In a production environment, the type of camera, the lens, and lighting conditions influence the quality of data.

- For light-colored fabrics, additional front lighting attached to the textile machine was required to obtain accurate data. For dark-colored fabric, both front lighting and back lighting were necessary.
- Automatic camera calibration, depending on the surrounding lighting, was a challenge. The camera aperture had to be manually changed depending on the lighting conditions.
- Data capture using videos attached to the textile machine also resulted in distortion and chromatic aberration. Additional hardware had to be attached to the textile machine to obtain quality data.

Incorrect Power Supply for Textile Machine

- The textile machine was built with the U.S. power supply in mind. Since the solution was to be demonstrated in China, the machine manufacturer tweaked the power supply. However, due to incorrect wiring, machine cables caught fire, and the team had to wait four days for the technician to resolve the issue and get the machine restarted.

Integration

- Integration of the textile machine with cameras, lighting panels, and supported hardware is required for the accurate functioning of the entire solution.

Software with AI/ML

Data Collection

- The quality of data determines the quality of models. In order to remotely generate and test models, defects need to be simulated, which requires some domain knowledge to understand the different type of defects.
- Because textile machines are expensive, prototypes may have to be developed to accurately collect data for training and testing.

Data Labeling and Pre-Processing

- Some amount of domain knowledge is necessary for identifying and classifying the fabric defects correctly. Either a domain expert or ample research is required to understand the variety of different textile defects in order to build solutions to automate the textile defect detection process.

- Samples of good fabric and defective fabric are needed to develop accurate models. Unavailability of either will result in computer vision–based pre-processing of images that can result in lower-resolution images. This, in turn, can impact the model accuracy.
- Augmentation techniques may be used to increase the dataset. However, this can lead to generating more erroneous data, which can impact the accuracy of the defect detection solution.

Model Training

- The model generated is not scalable; that is, it needs to be trained for every fabric that varies in color, texture, or pattern.
- The model works with high accuracy on fabrics with simple patterns and colors. When the model was trained on white fabric, it worked on cream-colored fabric but failed for brown fabric.
- Slow network connectivity at the factory location can result in increased time for data upload and training.

Inference

- The average inferencing speed was 60 frames per second. However, when the speed of the fabric-rotating motor increased, the camera couldn't process all the incoming frames and was dropping some of them. This resulted in lower accuracy.
- The system was not robust enough to handle inferencing at a higher motor speed.
- Network slowness hampered the software installation process and inferencing speed.

Currently, industry is using cutting-edge technologies in IoT, computer vision, and AI/ML to solve different problems in various domains. In this case study, I have illustrated the use of these technologies by the textile industry to detect defects in fabrics.

Several computer vision–based algorithms and AI/ML techniques have been developed to automate the fabric inspection process. However, real-world implementation challenges have prevented their adoption in the industry.

Future solutions can be built by focusing on these customer-centric implementation problems. That could promote faster adoption of these solutions, thus improving product quality and reducing labor costs through automated textile defect detection.

Neethu Elizabeth Simon is an IoT/ML software engineer at Intel Corporation in the Internet of Things group, where she is responsible for the development and successful productization of smart end-to-end IoT products and solutions. She is currently focused on building scalable and production-ready smart vision–based solutions using machine learning concepts. Apart from work, Neethu is passionate about promoting girls in STEM, women in technology, and diversity and inclusion. She leads the Intel India-AZ Employee Resource Group to help create a culture of inclusion and support employee recruitment, retention, and progression efforts by aligning with Intel's Global Diversity & Inclusion Goals. Outside of work, Neethu leads the Arizona SWENext club, volunteers with Education Empowers Inc. in promoting STEM education, and has coached several students for various STEM-based robotics and IoT competitions. She and her team of STEM volunteers were recognized with the 2019 SWE Motorola Foundation Multicultural Award for demonstrating the highest level of diversity, inclusion, and outreach. Neethu also likes public speaking and has presented at multiple conferences, including the Women in Analytics Conference and the Society of Women Engineers Conference.

References

[1] "Gartner Identifies Top 10 Strategic IoT Technologies and Trends." Press release, 7 November 2018 (https://www.gartner.com/en/newsroom/press-releases/2018-11-07-gartner-identifies-top-10-strategic-iot-technologies-and-trends).

[2] Textile Handbook. Hong Kong Cotton Spinners Association, 2001 (https://www.worldcat.org/title/textile-handbook/oclc/47822055).

[3] "Defects Glossary." CottonWorks, n.d. (https://www.cottonworks.com/resources/defects-glossary/).

[4] Howard, Andrew G., et al. "MobileNets: Efficient Convolutional Neural Networks for Mobile Vision Applications." arXiv, 17 April 2017 (https://arxiv.org/abs/1704.04861).

[5] OpenVINO (https://software.intel.com/content/www/us/en/develop/tools/openvino-toolkit.html).

Jenn Schilling
Data Analyst
University of Arizona

Making a Difference with Data Viz

Creating an impactful and effective data visualization is a challenge, but when done successfully, graphs and charts can make a significant difference in the real world. It is hard to tell a story or see patterns in numbers in a spreadsheet. Sometimes the sheer volume of data makes it impossible to see progress or growth in an organization. I enjoy working with data visualization to help people make sense of their data and see the story in numbers.

In my work as a consultant, I have had the opportunity to work with the Arizona Commission for Postsecondary Education (ACPE). I began working with this organization a little more than two years ago when it was beginning an initiative to increase completion of the Free Application for Federal Student Aid (FAFSA). Students complete the FAFSA each year to apply for grants and loans from the federal government. Many institutions of higher education also use the FAFSA to grant need-based scholarships and awards to students. Completing the FAFSA is a key indicator of a student's intentions to begin postsecondary education and a critical step along that path.

Currently, Arizona ranks 49th in the United States in FAFSA completion by high school seniors. Millions of dollars in grant money are left on the table each year as a result of students not completing the application.

A Call to Action

A few years ago, the Arizona Governor's Office of Education, the nonprofit education alliance Achieve 60AZ, and the ACPE partnered together and issued a call to action by establishing the Arizona FAFSA Challenge. This statewide initiative aims to increase FAFSA completion among Arizona high school seniors. An important step in this initiative was to develop a centralized, public way to track FAFSA completion rates for Arizona high schools. Without the data on FAFSA completion rates, the Arizona FAFSA Challenge would not have a way to monitor statewide improvement or provide schools with key metrics on their progress toward the goal of increasing FAFSA completion.

I was brought on as a consultant to develop a centralized, state-level system that would track FAFSA completion rates and display the data in a meaningful way to state, community, and high school stakeholders. The Arizona FAFSA Challenge dashboard would provide a vital resource for high school staff, administrators, and community stakeholders to view the FAFSA completion progress for the state and for the 429 individual Arizona high schools included in the data.

Prior to the creation of the dashboard, Arizona did not have a centralized location that housed FAFSA data for the state's high schools. This made it difficult to publicly track FAFSA completion trends and data for the more than 400 high schools in Arizona. Without the dashboard, each individual school and college access organization in the state would have to visit a federal government website and pull its own weekly FAFSA data as raw numbers. The ACPE and its partners likewise lacked a straightforward way to visualize FAFSA completions.

Working collaboratively with the ACPE, I created the Arizona FAFSA Challenge dashboard (https://fafsachallenge.az.gov/dashboard), which went into production for the 2018-2019 school year. Now receiving an estimated 4,000 views a month, the FAFSA Challenge dashboard has made a positive impact on the state since its launch two years ago. It is utilized by schools statewide and has gained national attention from other state education organizations that are in the planning stages of creating their own state FAFSA dashboards. More importantly, the dashboard has achieved the goal of bringing attention to the importance of the FAFSA and has motivated high schools and school districts to establish internal FAFSA completion goals. The dashboard provides schools with the detailed information they need about current and past-year FAFSA completion rates by week, which allows them to better target FAFSA initiatives and track their improvement.

The Importance of Visualizing Data

My work on the Arizona FAFSA Challenge dashboard has shown me how important it is to visualize data.

First of all, without this dashboard, many schools would not have access to their FAFSA completion data, so they would be unable to set meaningful goals for FAFSA completion and monitor their progress week to week as they hold FAFSA events and the senior class moves toward graduation. The dashboard has also highlighted the FAFSA's importance by being housed on a state website and providing data on FAFSA completions at the state, district, and school level. Without the dashboard, the FAFSA completion rate data would not be getting such high focus.

Second, the dashboard allows users to compare schools and districts to one another, something that is nearly impossible to do with the data in its raw format, as it is presented in state-level spreadsheets with one week's worth of data at a time. Now that I have developed a system for the ACPE to update the backing data for the dashboard, schools can view their completion rates week to week and compare their data over different school years. The framework I created for the dashboard makes this possible, but the visualizations are equally important, as they show the data in a clear and effective way that helps the viewer see patterns and track improvement.

Finally, I discovered through this project how powerful data visualization can be, especially for stakeholders who do not have regular access to effective graphs and charts. Working with the ACPE and its partner schools, I was able to get feedback from users of the dashboard as I developed it. The users were thrilled to see FAFSA completion data in a new, user-friendly way, and they also provided useful feedback on how to make the dashboard clearer for users unfamiliar with data.

With effective data visualization, change can be made. The state of Arizona has been able to monitor FAFSA completion rate progress in a way it would not be able to without data visualization. Without the ability to visually track this data, high schools, school districts, and community stakeholders would not have an awareness of FAFSA completion, nor would they be able to see their metrics. By highlighting patterns and allowing people to view their data in ways that would not be possible without graphs and charts, data visualization can make a difference.

Jenn Schilling is currently a data analyst in the University Analytics and Institutional Research department at the University of Arizona in Tucson. Prior to joining the University of Arizona, Jenn taught middle school for two and a half years. She also served as an AmeriCorps Vista member, working in college access. Before turning to education, Jenn spent four years working in industry as an operations research engineer in the supply chain at Intel and then as a statistician in the advertising and market research industry.

Jenn is passionate about increasing access to and improving equity in education, STEM fields, and the tech industry, and she believes strongly in the power of data and analytics to bring attention to inequities. Jenn has worked on freelance projects in data visualization, including the Arizona FAFSA Challenge Dashboard. Jenn also enjoys teaching and sharing her knowledge on data literacy, data visualization, personal finance, math education, and personal development.

Jenn holds an MS in computational operations research from the College of William and Mary and a BS in applied mathematics with a minor in computer science, also from the College of William and Mary. She also has a certificate in secondary education and teaching.

Emily Buser
Business Intelligence Analyst
Columbus Metropolitan Library

Analytics in the Time of Covid-19

Inevitably when I encounter someone who asks me what I do for a living, and I mention that I work in a public library, I'll get one of two reactions: they'll tell me how much their family enjoys their local library, or they'll say how much they enjoyed going to the library as a child. Given that I'm not a librarian, the next question usually is, "Then what exactly do you do?" When I state I'm an analyst, that's when their eyebrows rise and their curiosity is truly piqued. What would an analyst be doing at a public library?

Those of us who work in data analysis do so because we value the process of exploration and discovery. Working at a public library — and more specifically, an organization that serves a diverse community — has truly yielded a wealth of professional growth opportunities for me. During my tenure, it's been my experience that public libraries strive to continuously examine their programs and services in order to meet a wide range of community needs. Oftentimes these needs will extend beyond the traditional view many might hold of public libraries as "book repositories." In fact, libraries can serve as meeting spaces for groups, resources for school projects, safe havens for after-school hours, touchpoints for connections to local social services, and business centers offering computer or wireless access, to name a few.

Reimagining "Open to All" During a Pandemic

As the needs of communities change, the ability of libraries to meet those needs successfully depends in part on how well they are able to adapt and adjust. This has been incredibly important during the Covid-19 pandemic; libraries were not unique in being challenged to face a "new normal," one that seemed to change almost daily. Suddenly the motto of "Open to All," a phrase that appears above the entrance of our main library in downtown Columbus, Ohio, needed to be redefined and reimagined. Like all businesses and organizations open to the public, libraries weren't immune to the widespread shutdowns that occurred nor the need to develop safe reopening plans.

Because of the Covid-19 pandemic, one of my research projects this year was to investigate whether the Columbus Metropolitan Library (CML) could utilize any publicly available community data sets to help inform its plans for reopening and safely serving the community. As someone who had no prior career knowledge of public health data, I was starting from square one in my journey.

While there were certainly numerous data points mentioned and cited by the media, such as infection rates, I couldn't decipher how these data types might fit into the library universe. I needed to better define my research question in order to focus my search. After a bit more investigation, I realized that what I really wanted to discover was whether any data sets existed that might shed light on the social and/or economic impact of the Covid-19 crisis on communities in our area.

With this question in mind, I came to a few decisions before I started my data exploration. First, if the library was to use this information in any strategic or informative manner, I needed the data to be credible and from a reliable source I could trust. Second, I had to feel confident that I had a basic understanding of what I was examining. To my mind, having access to a data dictionary or documentation was a required element. If thorough documentation didn't exist, I was going to look for another avenue. Third, I needed to present this data in a manner that would be digestible for my audience. I wanted my analysis to be succinct yet also comprehensive enough to be understood and hopefully applicable to any decision-making for CML.

What I discovered was a dataset created and maintained by the Centers for Disease Control and Prevention (CDC)/Agency for Toxic Substances and Disease Registry. More specifically, the CDC's Geospatial Research, Analysis, and Services Program (GRASP)[1] developed an index to effectively measure a community's social vulnerability, down to the census tract level. The CDC defines social vulnerability as the "resilience of communities when confronted by external stresses on human health, stresses such as natural or human-caused disasters, or disease outbreaks," further stating that "Reducing social vulnerability can decrease both human suffering and economic loss."[2] How resilient communities are to these types of events can be measured via its Social Vulnerability Index, which is created with 15 different U.S. Census variables.

Not only did the CDC make this indexed data available for download, but the agency paired it with geospatial data to allow for mapping. Using Tableau, I was able to map this data and overlay CML's locations, which gave me the ability to see where our locations fell in terms of socially vulnerable populations. If a library branch is located in the darker-shaded areas, that could indicate increased public need for library services as well as increased vulnerability to environmental stressors such as Covid-19. What resulted from my mapping was a one-page summary document, which could be shared with various library stakeholder groups to inform their decision-making.

While these data points were 2018 estimates from the U.S. Census, I believe the map still afforded CML the opportunity for additional reflection and highlighted aspects to consider when developing reopening plans for the public. These included not just what initial services we should prioritize, but also what other precautions we'd need to consider in order to keep our staff and customers safe during the pandemic. While the summary document was just one element of analysis that fed into the larger spectrum of data and policies examined by CML during its reopening decision-making and planning, I believe it made an important contribution.

Emily Buser joined the Columbus Metropolitan Library (CML) in 2014 as its business intelligence analyst. In this role, she works on a variety of analytic and research projects to help support CML's programs and services for its customers. Prior to this role, Emily served as a policy and research analyst for nearly 10 years within the Office of Policy and Accountability at the Ohio Department of Education. She received a BBA in marketing with a concentration in the Hesburgh Program for Public Service from the University of Notre Dame and an MEd in education from the Harvard Graduate School of Education. Currently she resides in Columbus, Ohio, along with her two cats and husband, prioritized in that order.

References

[1]"CDC SVI Data and Documentation Download." Centers for Disease Control and Prevention/ Agency for Toxic Substances and Disease Registry/Geospatial Research, Analysis, and Services Program, last reviewed 15 September 2020 (https://www.atsdr.cdc.gov/placeandhealth/svi/ data_documentation_download.html).

[2] "At A Glance: CDC Social Vulnerability Index (SVI)." Centers for Disease Control and Prevention/Agency for Toxic Substances and Disease Registry/Geospatial Research, Analysis, and Services Program, last reviewed 5 February 2020 (https://svi.cdc.gov/index.html).

Chloe Page
Postdoctoral Researcher
University of Pittsburgh

Data Science and a Paradigm Shift for Psychiatry

The mental health field is moving toward a paradigm shift in our understanding of psychiatric illness. Neuroscience is advancing knowledge about the inner workings of the brain and changes in genes, cells, and circuits that contribute to mental illness, while psychology continues to refine behavioral and sociological perspectives on pathology. Data science is needed to integrate these approaches and build the models that will shift away from discrete diagnostic categories based solely on behavioral symptoms and toward a multidimensional understanding of mental health and disease.

Historically, as well as in the present day, the Diagnostic and Statistical Manual of Mental Disorders (DSM) has guided the classification and diagnosis of conditions such as depression, anxiety, and schizophrenia. Now in its fifth edition, the DSM approaches mental disorders as categories and subcategories defined by behavioral symptoms. For example, major depressive disorder (MDD) is a diagnostic category that resides under the "depressive disorders" classification. To meet the criteria for a diagnosis of MDD, one must exhibit five or more behavioral symptoms (such as anhedonia, low mood, suicidal thoughts or behavior, or sleeping more/less) out of a list of eight descriptive possibilities during the same two-week period.

Thinking Beyond the Box

Psychiatry has relied on this "box" model of mental disorders since 1952, when the first edition of the DSM was published. However, advances in neuroscience — as well as the realities of the lived experience of mental illness — have exposed many of the limitations of placing behavioral symptoms into discrete diagnostic boxes. Many disorders are comorbid with each other, such as depression and anxiety or depression and autism, relationships that are not readily clear according to the DSM categories. Perhaps most importantly, the DSM box model focuses solely on behavioral manifestations of a disorder for diagnoses, to the exclusion of other predictors ranging from the genetic to the sociological.

With these limitations in mind, the National Institute of Mental Health (NIMH) launched in 2010 an initiative called the Research Domain Criteria (RDoC) project. RDoC is an ambitious yet necessary effort to integrate neurobiological, behavioral, and demographic features of mental health into comprehensive models of pathology. Instead of categorizing illnesses into diagnostic boxes, RDoC aspires to a "domain" model of mental illnesses where conditions are understood as dysfunctions across domains of brain systems and behavior. RDoC is continuously evolving, and at the time of this writing encompasses six domains:

1. Negative valence systems
2. Positive valence systems
3. Cognition
4. Social processing
5. Arousal/regulatory systems
6. Sensorimotor systems

The depression symptom of anhedonia, for instance, may be understood as disruptions in positive valence systems with biological dysfunction (impaired dopamine transmission, dysfunctional reward pathways in the brain) and behavioral manifestations.

Advantages of the RDoC approach include the ability to build an understanding of the relationship between different disorders (e.g., the similarities between depression and anxiety) and integrate biological and behavioral information. At present, an RDoC-based understanding of mental illness has not been employed for diagnosis and treatment, but scientists and clinicians are collaborating to build these multidimensional models of neuropsychiatric conditions.

How Data Science Can Help

Within this model-building endeavor, there is a much-needed role for data scientists to play in integrating RDoC domains (negative valence, etc.) and levels of analysis (genetics, behavior, etc.). For example, an analytic approach with great potential for psychiatry is unbiased clustering. In genetics, unbiased clustering can be used to group similar cells together based on their gene expression profiles. In psychiatry, unbiased clustering could be similarly applied to group patients together based on their symptom profiles, including biological and behavioral symptoms.

Using this approach, one can envision t-distributed stochastic neighbor embedding (t-SNE) plots where spatially arranged clusters of patients represent the relationships between patterns of symptoms. Such a t-SNE plot might even be able to parse heterogeneity in a disorder like depression by identifying clusters of patients, closely related in space on the plot, who have a strong genetic component to their symptoms versus those whose condition is more attributable to stress or trauma. Further heterogeneity could also be revealed, such as similarities between depression patients who sleep more compared to those who sleep less. Patients with anxiety symptoms would likely cluster near or within depression-related clusters, highlighting the close relationship between these two conditions. Unbiased clustering and dimensionality reduction analyses built from scientific and clinical data have the potential to transform the way we delineate boundaries between mental health conditions, which may also revolutionize treatment approaches and pave the way for personalized, precision psychiatry.

Neuropsychiatric disorders may also be able to be modeled in silico using advanced data analytic and simulation techniques. Disorders such as depression, autism, and schizophrenia are increasingly being thought of as network disorders that must be comprehended as complex interactions between various regions of the brain and the connections and activity of neurons within those brain regions. For example, depression may be a network disorder with disrupted activity and connectivity between regions like the prefrontal cortex (cognitive processing and emotional regulation), the amygdala (positive and negative valence assignments), and the basal ganglia (reward processing), among others. Computational approaches can simulate these networks and mathematically alter parameters such as the number and strength of connections between neurons, the number of neurons within a network, and the activity of these neurons.

The Rewiring Brain: A Computational Approach to Structural Plasticity in the Adult Brain, edited by Arjen van Ooyen and Markus Butz-Ostendorf, contains numerous examples of such mathematical models for simulating network plasticity and activity with implications for understanding stroke or brain lesion pathology and recovery. However, similar mathematical models have been sparsely applied to neuropsychiatric disorders. Simulations of network function and dysfunction could transform our understanding of how mental pathology transpires in the brain.

As science moves more toward open data sharing, there are growing information repositories that data scientists can utilize. There is also a need for data scientists to streamline the organization of and access to these data repositories. For example, the NIMH Data Archive (NDA) hosts datasets from RDoC-inspired studies that include imaging, clinical, and omics (genomics, transcriptomics, proteomics) data. These open source datasets, together with ongoing scientific and clinical research studies, provide the foundations for building models of neuropsychiatric conditions.

The mental health field has long struggled with incomplete understandings of pathology, arbitrary diagnostic delineations, and trial-and-error approaches to treatment. A scientifically informed paradigm shift in mental illness diagnosis and treatment could improve outcomes for millions of patients. Data science is vital in this endeavor to integrate biological and behavioral variables across domains of brain systems and behavior.

Dr. Chloe Page is a neuroscientist researching the mechanisms of mental health conditions like depression and anxiety, as well as the basic biology of how we experience and process emotions. Her work has been published in peer-reviewed journals including Neuroscience, Scientific Reports, Neuroscience & Biobehavioral Reviews, and Genes, Brain and Behavior. *Outside of the academy, her passions include mental health awareness and destigmatization, gender and racial equity, and reading and writing as much as possible.*

Sunny (Sandhya) Patel
People Analytics Leader
Target

If You Build It ... They Will Come

Seven years ago, I enabled the human resources department at Cardinal Health to fundamentally change the way they respond to their customers by establishing the People Analytics and Insights team. This team empowered HR with information and analytics that allowed them to have straightforward data-based conversations and decisions. This proved to be a game changer.

Playing Small Ball

To provide context, the healthcare services industry has a known culture of moving slower for a myriad of reasons, including — but not exclusive to — politics, regulations, disparate data, and large complex systems that do not align. Innovation in healthcare services companies tends to be about creating efficiencies and typically is met with multiple roadblocks to adoption. Healthcare HR suffers the same symptoms and is also reliant on consensus-driven decisions, which at times is important because of the underlying attention to employee privacy and regulations, but nonetheless slows things down. As a result, innovation is not quick or easy.

When I joined HR at Cardinal, I was hired to build the HR analytics team. The folks in HR were well aware they had lots of interesting data and wanted to be more informative to leaders. They said they wanted insights, but I very quickly realized that what they wanted was pretty reporting on perfect data. This was not unlike many organizations early in the analytics maturity curve. To some extent, it was a valid expectation because providing reliable data in a consumable way is part of HR analytics.

Unfortunately, the focus became much more on cleaning data than it was translating it, and this consumed my time. I wasn't sure that they expected me to do anything different or whether they were aware of the possibilities. It didn't feel like they were really asking any questions, which is where analytics begins. However, I saw the problem and the potential, and I knew we had to think bigger.

At that time, the tumultuous healthcare industry was experiencing change from all directions that would impact our business model and our people. For our organization to prepare for more regulation and cost compression, we had to have a better handle on our organization's greatest expense and asset: our employees. We needed to have a deeper understanding of who worked for us, who should work for us, and how to leverage them to drive business results. It was important for HR to have a better line of sight to their population, be able to maximize and align their processes and programs, and provide measurements to monitor and change behavior.

I knew that, with analytics, HR could become key strategic partners in decisions regarding our business. I had done my due diligence to monitor the HR industry, talking to other companies and pioneers that were experts in the field. I began to generate my own roadmap of what needed to happen to transform our HR operational reporting to HR strategic analytics. I believed I could enable HR to be nimble and informed about our people. I knew it had to change, I knew it was time, and I knew that no one else had the vision for it. I decided to act and figure out how to create something impactful.

Showing HR How to Think Big

Scanning my environment, I identified a few barriers to overcome. My challenge was twofold. I had to change hearts and minds to believe that HR analytics was a strategic value to the organization, not just another "efficiency" in HR operations. First, I had to get leadership buy-in to get the funding to build capability to help deliver results. Second, I had to build capability and deliver results to get leadership buy-in and funding. Clearly this was a case of the chicken and the egg, so I just decided to do both at the same time.

232

I needed advocacy.

I was able to convince my leader that we should go to an industry conference together to see how we compared to others and learn what they were
doing. I knew this would be an eye-opening experience. Once she saw what
the potential was, my leader started to listen to my ideas from a different
perspective. She saw the opportunities we could work on. For example, we
could perform analysis to help us predict who would leave our organization
and why. This would enable us to assess our programs' return on investment
and use that to refine spending. We could better understand the movement
of our talent and whether we are building or buying effectively. We could
build dashboards for our HR business partners and prepare them with what
they needed to move past transactional conversations. After numerous discussions, she shifted reporting alignment and had me report directly to her to
move the agenda forward and attract the CHRO's attention to the potential
of the work and secure some funding to begin.

Around the same time, I had the chance to present to the top leaders of the
organization a new idea that would help to solve a problem, advance the
organization, or streamline a process. I presented on "Changing how HR
informs the organization, using analytics and information to drive change
and innovation." With some examples from the movie *Moneyball*, I ran them
through a scenario that demonstrated how objectively understanding talent
through analytics could allow us to leverage employee strengths and skills
to create innovative project teams. At the time, I didn't have many real facts
and almost chose another project, but I presented this idea in order to create
awareness and pull. If senior leaders had no idea of what we were trying to
do in HR, they would never have changed their expectations and therefore
never pushed us with questions.

I was on my way to getting leadership buy-in with funding and began to
deliver small wins. We started by revamping high-visibility deliverables. A big
early win was revamping a presentation that went to our organization's top
20 leaders. We converted 30 pages of information that showed metrics on

how well HR was executing to four pages of relevant information about our organization's talent. Rather than providing running list of activities completed, the presentation focused on the work HR did that impacted the operations of the business. I tried to make the deliverable captivate my audience.

Forming My Dream Team

As funding got approved, I began to build a team. I knew I wanted a team that brought different analytical skill sets and perspectives. From my experience, I found that fostering excellence and high quality, enabling people to use the diverse skills you hired them for, and working toward a common goal always resulted in a great team. Over two years, I hired an analyst with advanced stats, data modeling skills, and a research background; a supply chain analyst who was great at details, analytical thinking, and dissecting questions and process; a visualization guru who could build dashboards and make information translatable to different audiences; and a data geek with a strong skill set in data blending and systems. All of them were curious and engaged in our goal. I laid out the mission for the team: to use our unique expertise in HR to explore data, empower and enlighten others, and ultimately enable strategy.

Once I drafted a roadmap for the team, we delivered more results and fostered a curiosity that made people ask us more questions. Before we could reach the ideal state, where people asked project-worthy questions, we needed to put the answers to the basics at their fingertips. We did this by creating dashboards for all HR business partners and the Centers of Excellence, (Recruiting, Talent Management, Leadership Development, Diversity, etc). This empowered them and stimulated more interesting questions, which is where we could be more impactful. I knew that we were influencing a culture shift and it wouldn't happen overnight, so I spent the next few years pushing new ideas, consulting, teaching, and delivering results.

Fast-forward to the present, my team's efforts have influenced the way HR approaches questions, now turning to data to provide solid recommendations. The team is relied upon to empower others with trusted information, consult on strategic decisions, and participate in large-scale enterprise projects. The team is accountable for the development of tools to enable HR to drive data-based decision making. The team is sought out to provide thought leadership regarding the entire employee life cycle from sourcing to hiring, engagement, diversity, movement, learning and development, pipeline effectiveness, succession planning, and retention. The team also serve as teachers around best data practices, such as remembering to baseline pilots, raising awareness of visualization misinterpretations, and avoiding drawing incorrect conclusions from correlations.

In conclusion, perseverance in creating this team and delivering results advanced HR's continued transformation to a data-driven culture and increased the department's ability to deliver at a faster pace to foster change. If you build it ... they will come!

Sunny Patel created the People Analytics and Insights function for Cardinal Health. Her team's focus is to provide insights that shape and drive organizational people strategy. This includes delivering solutions that empower HR to make data-based decisions, partnering and consulting to identify opportunities, and collaboratively solving problems with targeted analytics. Her experience includes utilizing analytics to provide strategic intelligence to the business and customer, translating the relevance of analytics by connecting to business strategies and outcomes, and building high-powered teams with analytical capabilities and discipline.

Sunny started her career in the retail industry at The Limited Brands and Bath and Body Works corporate offices, where she worked with operations and marketing data to provide metrics-driven decision support. She then moved to Cardinal Health, a Fortune 25 healthcare services company. For the last 21 years, she has served within the organization in a variety of business marketing, strategy, and analytical roles, both as an individual contributor and in management positions. In all roles she has built new capabilities, teams, or service offerings for the organization. Sunny recently joined Target Corporation to build a best-in-class People Analytics team.

Sunny earned a BS in marketing from The Ohio State University and later an MBA from Franklin University. She is certified by the Human Capital Institute as a Human Capital Strategist. She has served on The Conference Board's Human Capital Analytics Executive Council and the i4cp People Analytics board and contributed to several publications.

Avishan Bodjnoud
Information Management Officer
United Nations Peace Operations

Promoting Peacekeeping Efforts via Machine Learning: A New-Age Tool for Conflict Prevention

Violent acts of aggression and war kill hundreds globally on a daily basis. Beyond this human toll and loss of life, such conflicts often lead to displacement of the family unit — the foundation upon which communities and societies depend for stability and socioeconomic progress. The disruption and displacement caused by violent conflict often have wide-ranging and cascading effects within nation-states and regions that share borders. According to the United Nations' Secretary-General, "The human and financial costs of conflict are high and rising. Forced displacement is at the highest levels since the Second World War, and hunger is resurgent after years of decline."[1] Civilians always pay the highest price in such instances of state conflict.

Violent conflict is often preventable, particularly if action is taken early. Thus it is incumbent on globally minded agents of change, such as the UN, to shift their modus operandi from being reactionary entities to ones that espouse preventative measures in instances of emergent conflict.

Early warning analysis has traditionally relied on a limited set of data. However, in recent years, conflict analysis has become increasingly digitized, which has led to more revelatory conclusions about the effectiveness of early conflict resolution. International organizations such as the UN are relying more and more on digital technologies to predict conflict. Thanks to the large amount of data at our disposal, the advancement in development of machine learning algorithms, and increased computing power, analysts can now forecast eruptions of violence at the national and subnational levels and do so more accurately than ever.

Different sets of political, social, institutional, and economic variables are identified as potential correlates of violence and conflict. Hakim Chekirou of the Sorbonne notes that "conflicts, in general, are strongly influenced by the infant mortality rate which is an indicator that poverty triggers conflicts."[2] Conflict history, patterns of fatality among civilians, poverty, and distance to the nearest conflict are also included in models to forecast conflict.

Machine Learning Techniques for Conflict Prediction

The use of machine learning for peacekeeping and conflict prevention can involve a combination of supervised and unsupervised topic modeling. With supervised modeling, algorithms are developed using methodologies such as linear regression to estimate the weight of each variable that contributes to the final prediction. Once algorithms are developed, they are trained on a large amount of past data, then calibrated and tweaked by analysts and political affairs officers. The human element is crucial to ensure the accuracy of the predictive capacity. An iterative consultation and collaboration process between the political analysts and data scientists in developing the machine learning models leads to the most accurately predictive models.

The use of a single machine learning model to predict conflict might raise the risk of biases. A conflict forecasting model may be accurate for a specific geographic area, for example, but inaccurate for other areas; therefore it is important to test models under different conditions. There is also the risk that not all relevant variables will be included in developing an algorithm; thus the use of unsupervised topic modeling in conflict forecasting is helpful to ensure high quality of predictions. The random forest algorithm, which combines multiple decision trees trained with a variety of datasets, is one approach that is often used for conflict prediction. By using unsupervised machine learning algorithms, patterns that political analysts were not aware of may be revealed.

Data Inputs

Much of the data that political analysts need to be able to understand to prevent conflict is qualitative in nature. It is humanly impossible to listen to endless radio stations, read hundreds of thousands of tweets, and watch untold hours of video. By using natural language processing, however, it is now possible for data scientists to prepare unstructured data formats to feed machine learning models.

Data collection is often a resource-intensive task, especially in remote areas where the local population does not have access to the internet or more modern technology. Local radio stations are often the source of information required to understand the local perceptions on a certain topic, such as a peace process or an election. The anecdotes and opinions shared in local dialects can be turned into data formats that can be consumed by the early warning models. This information can help stop the spread of fake news or hate speech and the outbreak of violence.

As more people in the rural areas start getting online, social media listening and sentiment analysis methodologies can further be used to understand local perceptions. Currently, in certain parts of Africa, 80% of social media account users are men. This presents a serious challenge if one needs to understand the opinion of women and girls on a certain topic, such as safety and security. Data scientists need to be aware of gender biases within their datasets; there needs to be an equal and diverse participation of men and women of different ethnic groups when social media is used for conflict prevention.

Satellite imagery can be a further relevant data source. Data scientists can analyze satellite imagery using image recognition algorithms to look out for patterns of drought due to the negative impact of climate change, another indicator of destabilization. Democratization of satellite imagery has improved situational awareness and enhanced early warning models.

Conclusion

Human beings might not yet be at the point where we can accurately predict any upcoming conflict. Indeed, human beings might not ever be there due to the nature of mankind and the irrationality of violent conflicts. However, machine learning provides a tool that can warn humanitarian organizations and countries of the likely emergence of a conflict due to poverty, climate change, elections results, or a pandemic. Through the use of such early warning models, lives can be saved and resources can be used to improve the well-being of human beings.

Avishan Bodjnoud works at the United Nations, Department of Peace Operations. She supports leveraging data and analytics for evidence-based planning, analysis, and decision-making. Avishan previously worked at the United Nations, Department of Safety and Security, managing the global security databases and data-driven reporting system. Avishan holds an MS in information management engineering, an MA in Middle Eastern studies, and a BS in computer software engineering. She was an impact fellow at Singularity University in Silicon Valley. Avishan was nominated by the United Nations Office of Information Communication Technology as a STEM Role Model and is an advocate for diversity in analytics and machine learning. She was born and raised in Tehran, Iran.

References

[1]United Nations Secretary-General. "United Nations Secretary-General's Remarks at Security Council Meeting on Conflict Prevention and Mediation," 12 June 2019 (https://www.un.org/sg/en/content/sg/statement/2019-06-12/secretary-generals-remarks-security-council-meeting-conflict-prevention-and-mediation-delivered).

[2]Chekirou, Hakim. "Predicting Future Wars." *Towards Data Science*, 26 June 2020 (https://towardsdatascience.com/predicting-future-wars-7764639f1d8d).

ABOUT THE CURATORS

Rehgan Avon

Rehgan founded Women in Analytics in 2016 with the hope of providing more opportunities for diverse voices to be heard in the analytics space. This past year she launched a company, Ikonos Analytics, with her co-founder in order to help organizations learn best practices around building and using AI. Her passion is driven by designing AI around the user and understanding the intended or unintended consequences of AI. She has worked at multiple startups in the analytics space, designing technology to support the complex process of building and deploying models.

Dave Cherry

Dave Cherry, principal of Cherry Advisory, LLC, is a thought leader, executive strategist, and speaker. He helps clients in the customer experience industry (that's everyone with customers) define a customer experience strategy enabled by innovation and measured/informed by analytics that drives deep relationships and connections with customers.

He was an attendee at the first Women in Analytics conference, joining the WIA Advisory Board shortly thereafter. Over the last three-plus years in that role, he's helped to guide the strategic direction, build corporate support and secure sponsors, and promote and support the WIA community.

Dave is also a member of the International Institute of Analytics Expert Panel, serves on three additional advisory boards (CbusRetail, CCAD Retail Advisory, and Mive), and is the co-producer of the Digital Solutions Gallery at the Ohio State University. Each of these affiliations helps Dave connect with a broader audience and help spread the mission of WIA.

Throughout his career, Dave has worked with and for leading organizations such as LBrands, Polo Ralph Lauren, Easton Town Center, ascena Retail Group, Journeys, DSW, Disney, Alliance Data, Nationwide Insurance, AEP, Huntington Bank, Cardinal Health, OhioHealth, Deloitte Consulting, and Price Waterhouse. He holds a BS in economics from The Wharton School at the University of Pennsylvania.

Made in the USA
Las Vegas, NV
22 July 2022